MENU

**METROPOLITAN
OPERA
COMPANY**

Best Wishes —
[signature]
Atlanta — April 23-1925.

THE
METROPOLITAN
OPERA
COOKBOOK

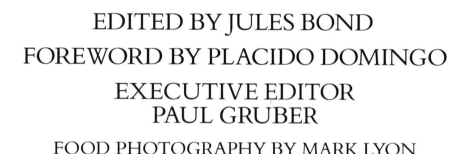

EDITED BY JULES BOND

FOREWORD BY PLACIDO DOMINGO

EXECUTIVE EDITOR
PAUL GRUBER

FOOD PHOTOGRAPHY BY MARK LYON

STEWART, TABORI & CHANG
METROPOLITAN OPERA GUILD
NEW YORK

Recipes by Bonelli, Lehmann, Melchior, Milanov, Swarthout, Thorborg, Tibbett, and Traubel copyright © 1941 Prentice-Hall, Inc.

Recipes by Cossotto, Kubiak, Nucci, Pavarotti, Rysanek, Schenk, Scotto, Tavela, and Weikl copyright © 1975, 1977, 1982, 1985, 1987 Metropolitan Opera Guild, Inc.

Due to limitations of space, sources of illustrations begin on page 235 and constitute an extension of this page.

The publisher gratefully acknowledges the assistance of Tiffany & Co.

Edited by Carole Berglie

Published in 1988 by
Stewart, Tabori & Chang, Inc.
740 Broadway
New York, New York 10003

Library of Congress Cataloging-in-Publication Data

The Metropolitan Opera cookbook / edited by Jules J. Bond ; foreword by Placido Domingo ; executive editor, Paul Gruber ; food photography by Mark Lyon.
    p. . cm.
    Includes index.
    ISBN 1-55670-039-3 : $30.00
    1. Cookery, International.   2. Metropolitan Opera (New York, N.Y.)—Miscellanea.
I. Bond, Jules Jerome.   II. Metropolitan Opera Guild.
TX725.A1M474   1988
641.5—dc19   88-15298
                                         CIP

Distributed by
Workman Publishing
708 Broadway
New York, New York 10003

Printed in Italy

10 9 8 7 6 5 4 3 2 1

PAGE 1: *Menu from the dining car of a 1940s Met tour train.* PAGES 2–3: *Atlanta was always one of the high spots of the annual Met tour, as the company was royally entertained by that city's citizens. Recognizable in this photo of a 1925 dinner are (clockwise from the head of the table) Lawrence Tibbett, Giuseppe de Luca, Antonio Scotti, Florence Easton, Frances Alda, Lucrezia Bori, Marion Telva, Edward Ziegler, Frances Peralta, Armand Tokatyan, Giovanni Martinelli, Clarence Whitehill, Julia Claussen, Rosa Ponselle, Léon Rothier, Kathleen Howard, Carlo Edwards, Tullio Serafin, Earle Lewis, and Jeanne Gordon.* FRONTISPIECE: *Sherry's Restaurant in the old Metropolitan Opera House.* OPPOSITE: *Spiro Malas as the Innkeeper in* Manon.

ACKNOWLEDGMENTS

The number of people involved with the preparation of The Metropolitan Opera Cookbook disproves the old adage about too many cooks spoiling the broth; in fact, it took almost as many hands to bring this book to completion as it does to stage an opera. (Fortunately, almost all of these recipes take less preparation time than it takes to hear the average opera.)

Our gratitude goes first to the many members of the Met family who took time to contribute recipes. We thank Maria Moore, Dorle Soria, Karen Kriendler Nelson, the family of Richard and Sara Tucker, and Jane Poole, all of whom tracked down rare recipes, and Prentice-Hall, Inc., for allowing us to include recipes that first appeared in their 1941 publication Favorite Recipes of Famous Musicians, by Charlotte S. Morris.

The Met's Director of Archives, Robert Tuggle, and his assistant, Dennis McGovern, were always helpful in finding both historic recipes and unusual illustrations, as were Mary Gene Sondericker and Paul Kindt.

The food photographs were themselves productions, and besides those credited in the back of the book, we wish to thank Lucine Amara, Roberta Peters, Regina Resnik, and Renata Scotto for generously loaning their personal properties for these photos. Our appreciation also goes to Arthur Ashenden and his prop department at the Met, who worked enthusiastically to gather the other props used, and to Gail Pam Frohlinger and Larry Riederman for their help.

Two of the Guild's good friends volunteered many hours on this project, and they deserve special thanks. Wally Riecker (often aided by her husband, Charlie) spent many hours petitioning, persuading, cajoling, and for all we know blackmailing singers to contribute recipes for publication. And Katie Brand contributed in many ways, from collecting recipes and correcting proofs to testing recipes. Both of these ladies worked several years on this project without ever losing their patience or gaining an ounce. Our thanks also go to Lucinda Frame and Kent Cottam for aiding in the testing of recipes.

This book would not have been published were it not for the enthusiasm and support of our co-publishers, Stewart, Tabori & Chang. The Guild's gratitude goes particularly to Andrew Stewart, Roy Finamore, and J.C. Suarès, who saw us through this project and helped make it a reality.

Jules Bond and Paul Gruber

OVERLEAF: *The* Porgy and Bess *picnic, with Charles Williams as Sportin' Life.*

CONTENTS

FOREWORD

I have sometimes been asked to write prefaces for books about opera, but I must admit that this is the first time I have ever been asked to write the preface to a cookbook! However, since this is the first cookbook that has ever been produced by the Metropolitan Opera, I suppose that Julia Child and Paul Prudhomme needn't worry about competition from me yet.

Seriously, I think the editors had a wonderful idea when they decided that the Met audience would like to have a cookbook from their opera house. There has always been a strong connection between opera and food; for instance, I have never heard of a dish named after a famous writer or actor or painter, but there are many recipes named after singers and composers. And, although you usually don't hear baseball fans or museum attendees discuss food, just ask an opera lover how he cooks pasta, and you have a guaranteed conversation of at least a half-hour. I think that opera lovers are usually romantic, emotional people who love life and therefore are interested in one of the great joys of living—food! And because people who are really interested in food are likely to know how to prepare it, most opera fans have learned their way around the kitchen.

I know that there are some people who don't care about food, but I find that difficult to understand. To me, eating has always been an important facet of life, not just something we do to stay alive. This is partly because of the way I was brought up—my grandmother ran a restaurant in Zaragoza, my father's hometown in Spain. It was called *La Viuda de Domingo*, or The Widow of Domingo. My mother is from a town called Guetaria, in Basque country, a fishing town with a great reputation for the magnificent *calamares, merluza*, shrimp, and clams that are caught there. Many of my early childhood memories have to do with food. One of my great passions as a boy was to eat *churros*, thin pieces of dough fried lightly in oil until they are crisp. We would buy them from street vendors and dunk them in hot chocolate, and I thought they were the most delectable treats ever created. I also have very strong memories of holiday meals, when the entire family would gather to celebrate and enjoy such treats as turkey stuffed with raisins and prunes, *cardos* (a delicious fried vegetable dish), *besugo* (whitefish), and for dessert, *turrones* (hard candy with nuts) and *mazapán* (a heavenly cake made with egg whites and sugar). I have tried to prepare paella, with good results, but it is so difficult I always keep some steaks in reserve, just in case!

I still feel that the most important time I spend with my family is around the dinner table. When we are all together at a meal the food becomes a backdrop for the talking. This is when my wife, Marta, and I find out what is going on in our sons' lives and what is on everyone's mind. The food is why we have come together, but much more happens besides eating.

There is a popular notion that opera singers indulge at the table, all the while reassuring themselves that they are only helping the voice. The truth is that for singers, gaining weight is an occupational hazard arising from two factors: we travel all the time and we work at night. Have you ever tried to lose weight on a vacation, or even a business trip? Restaurant food is always fattening, and there are invariably periods of boredom or tension when it is easy to overeat. Since most singers don't like to eat before a performance, and then must work very strenuously for three or four hours, we are usually famished by midnight, when we dine and then go to bed. It would be difficult to think of a better way to gain weight. We all know it's not healthy to be overweight, and good health is of primary importance if you want to maintain the kind of schedule a successful singer must have. I think it is the extremes of weight that must be avoided.

And so it becomes a difficult but necessary struggle for most of us to stay at our optimal weight. As you look through this book, you'll find very few recipes to help you do this; the artists and other contributors of recipes have given us a mouthwatering collection of great international dishes—most of us could gain ten pounds just reading this book. I'm very glad, by the way, that *The Metropolitan Opera Cookbook* includes not only recipes from singers, but members of the orchestra, chorus, ballet, staff, and even board members. Opera is a collaboration of many, many people, only a few of whom are famous or even seen on stage. I've worked at the Met for twenty years, and I know that many of those involved not only like to cook, but are wonderful cooks. I look forward to trying some of their recipes myself!

So get your chopping boards, your mixing bowls, and your whisks ready, and preheat your ovens. Put on your favorite opera recordings—*Tosca* or *Forza* are great for cooking to, and you can switch to *Traviata* later for a festive meal, or *Bohème* for a romantic dinner for two. Your guests will be amazed (and I hope suitably impressed) when you announce that the recipes for the evening's meal were given to you personally by Birgit Nilsson, Joan Sutherland, Leontyne Price, Luciano Pavarotti, and Plácido Domingo.

Buen provecho, bon appetito, bon appétit, guten apetit, and enjoy your meal!

Plácido Domingo

Turkey Pâté
Suzanne Laurence

Gravlax with Swedish Mustard Sauce
Birgit Nilsson

Tuna–Jalapeño Dip à la Andrade
Rosario Andrade

Kitty's Caviar "Au Père Jacques"
James Levine

Salmon Mousse
Mrs. Donald D. Harrington

Liptauer Cheese Spread
Erica Merkling

Chopped Chicken Liver
Sylvia Shapero

Crabmeat Salad Mousse
Robin Enoch-Horn

Stuffed Mushrooms
Elaine B. Kones

Ham Mousse
Jarmila Novotná

Meatballs Rievman
Ellen Rievman

Quiche à l'Oignon
Harold H. Healy, Jr.

Spanakopeta
Marilyn Horne

Baked Clams
Millicent Hacker

Ekstrom's Julglögg
Lenore Rosenberg

Cocktail de Lady Charles
Thomas J. Hubbard

The Ho-jo-to-ho Cure
Aage Haugland

PRECEDING PAGES: *Plácido Domingo and Ileana Cotrubas drink to love in* La Traviata. OPPOSITE: *The Opera Club at the Metropolitan Opera, Lincoln Center.* OVERLEAF: *Birgit Nilsson's Gravlax with Swedish Mustard Sauce, and the pistol she used in* Fidelio. *Miss Nilsson is shown as Brünnhilde.*

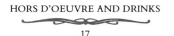
HORS D'OEUVRE AND DRINKS

Suzanne Laurence
Turkey Pâté

5 tablespoons unsalted butter
2 small yellow onions, chopped
2 large celery stalks, chopped
4 chicken or 2 turkey livers, cut up
½ pound fresh mushrooms, chopped
½ cup chopped cooked chestnuts (or unsweetened, canned)
½ cup dry Madeira (Sercial), dry sherry, or dry vermouth
⅛ teaspoon dried thyme
⅛ teaspoon powdered sage or poultry seasoning
Pinch of herbes de Provence (optional)
Salt and freshly ground black pepper to taste
1 teaspoon Worcestershire sauce
¾ cup chicken or turkey broth, approximately
1½ pounds raw turkey meat, cut up
2 eggs
1 cup fine white bread crumbs, approximately
Toast squares

In a skillet, melt the butter, add the onions and celery, and sauté over high heat for a few minutes. Add livers and sauté until celery is tender and the livers almost done, about 5 minutes. Add mushrooms and chestnuts and continue cooking. When the livers are fully cooked, in about another 3 minutes, add wine, then scrape and deglaze the skillet, dissolving the particles on the bottom of the pan. Add herbs and seasonings, Worcestershire, and about half the broth. Simmer for 1 minute, then remove from heat. Taste—the mixture should be highly seasoned and rather moist and mushy—add more broth if needed.

Place turkey in a food processor bowl and process until finely chopped. Add the cooked mixture, eggs, and enough breadcrumbs to just absorb the liquid. Pulse several times until well blended.

Preheat oven to 400 degrees. Line a 9 × 5-inch loaf pan with aluminum foil, then butter the lining. Fill the loaf pan with pâté mixture, and place pan in a larger baking dish. Fill dish with enough hot water to come halfway up the pan. Bake for 15 minutes, then reduce heat to 350 degrees and bake for another 1¼ hours.

Remove dish from oven and let pâté cool in the loaf pan. Place another pan filled with water on top of the pâté to weight it down as it cools and force out excess liquid. When cool, remove pâté from pan and slice. Serve cold, with toast squares. *Serves 6 to 8.*

Suzanne Laurence
is a dancer in the Metropolitan
Opera Ballet.

Birgit Nilsson
Gravlax with Swedish Mustard Sauce
MARINATED SALMON

Salmon
2 pounds center-cut salmon piece
3 tablespoons coarse (kosher) salt
½ cup sugar
10 white peppercorns, crushed
1 large bunch fresh dill, plus additional for
   garnish

Mustard Sauce
5 tablespoons sugar
2 tablespoons distilled white vinegar
1 (8-ounce) jar Swedish sweet mustard
6 tablespoons vegetable oil
6 tablespoons chopped fresh dill

Filet the salmon or have your fishmonger do it, leaving the skin on. Use tweezers or pliers to remove any remaining small bones. Mix salt, sugar, and pepper. Sprinkle some of this mixture in a dish just large enough to hold the filets. Add some of the dill sprigs and place one of the filets, skin side down, on top. Sprinkle filet with most of the remaining salt mixture, cover with remaining dill, top with the other filet (skin side up), and sprinkle with the remaining salt mixture. Cover fish with foil or a plate, and place a weight on top (for example, a large can of tomatoes). Refrigerate or keep in a very cool place for 36 hours, turning the salmon a few times

Birgit Nilsson at home.
ABOVE: *Some of the cast of the Georg Solti recording of Götterdämmerung celebrate its completion with a game of skat. Left to right are Thomas Stewart, Wolfgang Windgassen, Birgit Nilsson, Gottlob Frick, and Hans Hotter.*

while marinating. Baste filets with the juices that accumulate around the salmon.

While filets marinate, prepare the sauce. Dissolve sugar in vinegar, add mustard, and blend well. Stir in the oil and finally add the chopped dill.

When ready to serve, wipe the marinade off the filets and remove the skin. Cut salmon into thin diagonal slices. Cut skin into 1-inch strips, and sauté quickly—for a few seconds—in a hot, dry skillet. Garnish the salmon with sprigs of fresh dill and the sautéed skin strips. Serve with the traditional mustard sauce. *Serves 8.*

Birgit Nilsson
the great Wagnerian soprano, still lives in her native Sweden, on a farm near where she grew up as a child. "I hope the readers of the cookbook will love this dish as much as we do. I can't tell you how much salmon I have marinated last summer! Everyone loves it, and it is ready-made when the guests arrive." She adds, "If you want to filet the salmon yourself, here's how I do it. Clean and dry the salmon well, but do not rinse it. Divide it along the backbone, and remove all the bones carefully. Don't forget the fleshiest part of the back, and use a pair of pliers."

Rosario Andrade
Tuna–Jalapeño Dip à la Andrade

1 cup mayonnaise
2 (6½-ounce) cans tuna, drained well
1 bunch cilantro *(Chinese parsley or fresh coriander)*
1 medium onion
1–3 hot jalapeño peppers
Corn chips

Put all the ingredients except the jalapeños in a food processor and blend on high speed. Add a few jalapeños, taste, and add more as desired. Serve immediately with plain corn chips. *Serves 8 to 10.*

Note Jalapeño peppers are usually available fresh, or are sold canned or bottled in grades of mild, medium, or hot.

Rosario Andrade
was born in Vera Cruz, Mexico. She has sung Violetta, Mimi, and Arabella at the Met, and has also appeared in Mexico City, Glyndebourne, Chicago, and San Francisco. "My favorite recipes, like my favorite songs, were taught to me by my mother. I get the greatest joy in sharing both of these."

OPPOSITE: *Birgit Nilsson as Tosca.*

James Levine
Kitty's Caviar
"Au Père Jacques"

6 hard-boiled eggs
3 tablespoons mayonnaise
1½ cups chopped onions
8 ounces cream cheese, softened
¾ cup sour cream
4 ounces black caviar

Butter an 8-inch springform mold. In a bowl, chop the eggs and mix well with mayonnaise. Spread mixture in bottom of mold, then spread the onions on top of the egg mixture. Blend the cream cheese with the sour cream, and spread on top of the onions. Refrigerate overnight. When ready to serve, top mixture with caviar. *Serves 6 to 8.*

James Levine
was named Artistic Director of the Metropolitan Opera in 1986, having previously held the titles of Principal Conductor and Music Director. Since his Met debut in 1971, he has conducted more than 1,000 performances for the company, and continues to conduct at Salzburg and Bayreuth as well.
He tells us of this recipe:
"How appropriate to share a

recipe that I first enjoyed on the Met's annual spring tour. Several years ago, as Assistant Conductor of the Cleveland Orchestra, I discovered what was truly one of the greatest restaurants of the world— Au Père Jacques, located forty-five minutes from downtown Cleveland. It was run by Jack Schindler, a man of tremendous warmth, vitality, sensitivity, and talent who personally supervised every aspect of his incredible restaurant—from its superbly chosen and maintained wine cellar to the gourmet offering which included Tournedos Rossini and fresh sole that he could prepare in any of a hundred different variations—each described in glorious detail on the menu.

"Jack is also a music-lover, and he would often stay open late for us when the Met was in town, so I was able to introduce many of the company members to Au Père Jacques. There were numerous memorable evenings when six or eight of us would drive out to the restaurant after a performance to have dinner at midnight or one in the morning, and enjoy the best haute cuisine in a relaxed neighborhood atmosphere.

"Jack loves discovering the creations of other chefs, as well as developing new ones of his own, and

From a 1938 Met program.

he travels a great deal. In order to continue to travel and concentrate on his expanding wine shop, he decided to close the restaurant after having successfully run it for over twenty years. This is why the Met stopped going to Cleveland! No . . . but seriously, the prospect of going to Cleveland without being able to enjoy Jack's singular hospitality and style was not a happy thought. The first spring we were back, Jack asked me to dinner at his home with his wife and children, and invited me to bring several colleagues from the company. What a fantastic evening it was, and through their generosity and kindness our evening together became an annual event on the tour, and a highpoint of the season.

"The hors d'oeuvre offered by Jack's wife, Kitty, the first year we were at their home was such a favorite that I asked her for the recipe, and I've enjoyed it many times since. It's easy to make, festive in spirit, beautiful to look at, and delicious beyond belief. Now, each December during the holidays, we toast Kitty and Jack while enjoying caviar—their way. Bon appétit!"

Mrs. Donald D. Harrington
Salmon Mousse

1 envelope unflavored gelatin
½ cup boiling water
2 tablespoons lemon juice
1 small onion, sliced
½ teaspoon sweet paprika
1 teaspoon chopped fresh dill
1 (16-ounce) can red salmon, drained
1½ cups mayonnaise
1 pint heavy cream

Put gelatin in the bowl of an electric blender; add boiling water, lemon juice, and sliced onion and blend at high speed for about 40 seconds. Turn motor off. Add paprika, dill, salmon, and mayonnaise, then blend briefly at high speed. Add one-third of the cream at a time, blending a few times after each addition, then blend 30 seconds longer. Pour mixture into a 1½-quart mold and chill for at least 4 hours.

When ready to serve, unmold onto a chilled platter and garnish. *Serves 6 to 8.*

Mrs. Donald D. Harrington is a Managing Director of the Metropolitan Opera Association and has underwritten many new productions at the Met. In recognition of her generosity, the auditorium of the Metropolitan Opera has been named after her.

Erica Merkling
Liptauer Cheese Spread

3–4 large shallots
6 ounces soft goat cheese (if unavailable, use
*   farmer cheese)*
1 scant tablespoon Dijon mustard
1 generous tablespoon anchovy paste
1 tablespoon caraway seed
8 ounces cream cheese
2 tablespoons Hungarian sweet paprika
Capers, for garnish
Dark pumpernickel or rye bread, or crackers

Place shallots in a food processor and chop with the steel blade. Add goat cheese, mustard, anchovy paste, and caraway seed. Process and blend well. Add cream cheese and paprika, blending until very smooth. Taste mixture, and if a sharper taste is wanted, add a little more anchovy paste and mustard.

Place mixture in a glass dish or earthenware crock, garnish with capers, cover, and refrigerate for a day or so to blend flavors. Serve on dark pumpernickel or rye bread as an appetizer, or on crackers, with drinks. *Serves 6 to 8.*

Note If serving as a dip for crudités, thin mixture slightly with sour cream. Liptauer also makes an excellent sauce for fish when thinned with a little cream. Or put a dollop of liptauer on broiled or baked fish just before serving, and let it mingle with pan juices.

Erica Merkling
was the Art Director of Opera
News *magazine from 1947 to 1955.*
She is married to Frank Merkling,
who was Editor-in-chief of Opera
News *from 1957 to 1974.*

Heat fat in a skillet, add onion slices and sauté over low heat until onions are soft. Trim any fat from the livers, spread them on top of the onions, and continue cooking over low heat until the livers are just lightly browned but still pink inside; do not overcook them. Place contents of skillet, including any pan juices, in a chopping bowl. Add eggs and chop (by hand) until mixture is fluffy and egg whites are chopped into tiny pieces. Add grated onion and mayonnaise, season with salt and pepper, and blend well with a fork. Keep refrigerated, but let come to room temperature before serving. *Serves 6 to 8.*

Sylvia Shapero
is the slide librarian for the Metropolitan Opera Guild's Education Department. The wife of a surgeon, her recipe uses very little fat, but she notes that "those who are not diet-conscious may want to add two tablespoons of chicken fat."

Sylvia Shapero
Chopped Chicken Liver

1 tablespoon chicken fat or solid vegetable
  shortening
3 onions (a little smaller than tennis balls),
  thinly sliced
10 large chicken livers (about ¾ pound)
3 extra-large eggs, hard-boiled
1 tablespoon grated onion
½ tablespoon mayonnaise
Salt and pepper to taste

PRECEDING PAGES: L'Elisir d'Amore, *with (standing) Fernando Corena, Mirella Freni, and Mario Sereni.* LEFT: *Lucrezia Bori and Giovanni Martinelli.*

CATERING
300 PARK AVENUE
ESTIMATES

It was on October 22, 1883 that The Metropolitan Opera House opened ✦ Christine Nilsson's *Marguerite* brought forth a thousand "bravas" ✦ A brilliant company danced the old-fashioned waltz on the huge platform erected over the orchestra seats ✦ Louis Sherry served New York's select at supper, in the Opera House club rooms above ✦

Courtesy Lionel Mapleson Collection

Robin Enoch-Horn
Crabmeat Salad Mousse

½ cup mayonnaise, approximately
2 envelopes unflavored gelatin
¼ cup hot water
1 (10¾-ounce) can cream of mushroom soup
8 ounces cream cheese, softened
½ cup finely chopped celery
1 small onion, minced
¾ pound flaked crabmeat

Coat a 1-quart mold with mayonnaise. Sprinkle gelatin over hot water, let soften, then stir to dissolve. In a small saucepan, heat mushroom soup and cream cheese, stirring until smooth. Add celery, onion, and dissolved gelatin; stir, then fold in the crabmeat. Pour mixture into the mold, and chill overnight.

When ready to serve, unmold onto a chilled serving platter and garnish. *Serves 4 to 6.*

Robin Enoch-Horn
was an Administrative Assistant in
the Met's Finance Department.

Elaine B. Kones
Stuffed Mushrooms

1 pound large fresh mushrooms
3 tablespoons grated Parmesan cheese
2 cloves garlic, chopped
1 small onion, minced
1 cup fine dry seasoned bread crumbs
1 tablespoon minced fresh parsley
3 tablespoons butter, melted
Salt and pepper to taste
6 tablespoons olive oil

Preheat oven to 375 degrees. Remove mushroom stems and set caps aside. Chop and mix stems with remaining ingredients except olive oil and stuff the caps with the mixture. Pour 2 tablespoons oil in the bottom of a large baking pan. Put the mushrooms in the pan, stuffed side up. Spoon the remaining oil over the mushrooms, and bake until mushrooms are tender, about 15 minutes. Then place pan quickly under the broiler to brown tops. Serve at once. *Serves 4 to 6.*

Elaine B. Kones
is the Advertising Director for
Opera News *magazine.*

ABOVE: *From a Met program, 1931.* OPPOSITE: *Montserrat Caballé.*

Jarmila Novotná
Ham Mousse

2 envelopes unflavored gelatin
2 tablespoons Dubonnet
1 teaspoon lemon juice
½ cup hot chicken broth
2 eggs, separated
½ cup mayonnaise
5 dashes Tabasco
1 cup diced ham
½ cup heavy cream

In a blender bowl, put the gelatin, Dubonnet, lemon juice, and hot broth. Cover and blend at high speed for 1 minute. Add the egg yolks, mayonnaise, Tabasco, and ham and blend at high speed for about 20 seconds. Uncover container and, with the motor still running, gradually pour in the cream and blend for a few more seconds.

In a mixing bowl, beat the egg whites until stiff. Pour the ham mixture over the beaten egg whites and fold gently until well mixed. Pour into a 4-cup mold and chill until well set.

Unmold when ready to serve. Cumberland Sauce (page 169) goes well with the mousse. *Serves 4 to 6.*

Jarmila Novotná sang in her native Prague, in Berlin, in Vienna, and in Salzburg before coming to the Met in 1940. Well known for her beauty and acting ability as well as her singing, she sang for sixteen seasons at the Met, giving memorable performances as

A Star Stars in the Kitchen

1 After preparing mixture, braid four long strips of dough for bread base.

2 Two smaller rows are braided and placed pyramid-style on the base.

3 To finish her raisin bread, opera star Jarmila Novotna brushes braided dough with egg white and pops loaf into a moderate oven until it's nicely browned.

PHOTOS BY JOHN HEMMER, MIRROR MAGAZINE

By PRUDENCE PENNY

JARMILA NOVOTNA, an opera singer, a home maker, and a beauty, gave us our material for today.

Mme. Novotna was a protegee of Czechoslovakia's one-time President Masaryk and has had a great deal of fame in this country. But at heart she is a housewife and she really enjoys cooking good food and trading recipes. She made a raisin bread for us which she says usually was a holiday bread in her country but "in America every day is always a holiday." The recipe follows:

RAISIN BREAD
4 cups flour, sifted
½ cup sugar
1 tsp. salt
1 whole egg plus 2 yolks beaten together
1 cup milk
7 tbsps. melted butter or margarine
¼ cup lukewarm water
1 pkg. dry or compressed yeast
⅔ cups raisins, seedless
1 tsp. grated lemon rind
Resift flour into deep bowl with sugar

dough, then add the yeast slowly and mix dough until it doesn't stick. Cover bowl with a cloth and let dough rise in a warm place until double in bulk. This will take about 2 hours. Add raisins and lemon rind. Place dough on well floured board and divide into 9 portions, 4 large ones and 5 smaller ones. Roll each portion into a long thin roll between the hands. First braid the 4 large rolls and place on buttered pan. Next braid the 3 smaller rolls and place on top of the first one. Then place the last 2 rolls on top of the loaf to give it a nice shape. Let rise once more, brush with the white of an egg and bake in a moderate oven (350 degrees) for 50 minutes or until nicely done and brown.

A recipe for chicken which Mme. Novotna gave us is:

CHICKEN CLEMENCEAU
1 chicken, 1½ lbs.
8 tbsps. butter
1 cup green peas
2 medium potatoes, diced
6 mushrooms, diced
½ t

calibre is hen cooked with a fine wine. This is a recipe in keeping with the taste of a famous Caruso in whose movie Mme. Novotna recently worked. It follows:

CHAMPAGNE HEN
1 3-lb. hen
½ cup chopped celery
½ cup chopped mushrooms
2 chopped shallots
1 cup champagne
½ tsp. paprika
½ tsp. taragon
½ tsp. gelatine

Stuff the hen with a dressing made with the celery, mushrooms, shallot and taragon. Allow hen to stand for 12 hours and place in oven at 325 degrees F. for 1 hour. During the baking, baste with champagne until tender. Place in refrigerator to cool. Reduce stock and season with paprika. Stir in gelatine and pour mixture over hen and cool well before serving.

Octavian, Violetta, Cherubino, Mařenka, Antonia, and Orlovsky. Later she acted in television and films, including The Search. She lives in New York City. She recalls:

"I remember, in my childhood days, when my mother prepared the meals she always sang, and so in my memory cooking and music are synonymous. I learned not only many Czech folk songs this way, but also how to cook. Czech cuisine is rather rich, and its specialties include a variety of dumplings, some as a side dish for pork, venison, or other meat dishes, and others made with fruit fillings for dessert. I just adored apricot dumplings (see page 184), and after a good portion of crispy goose, I would eat about ten dumplings in one sitting—I simply forgot about my weight and enjoyed life. Another specialty is a raisin bread usually eaten at Christmas. 'Christmas' in Czech is Vanoce; that's how the bread got the name vanocka. It is served sliced for breakfast or for tea in the afternoon, with a little honey, apricot preserves, or just plain. Cooking is a very demanding art—time consuming, but enormously rewarding. A well-prepared meal, like a beautiful symphony, can lift your spirit."

Ellen Rievman
Meatballs Rievman

1½ cups bread crumbs
1 cup evaporated milk
2 pounds ground beef (chuck, sirloin, or other)
3 egg yolks
3 tablespoons chopped onion
2 teaspoons salt, or to taste
½ teaspoon black pepper
½ teaspoon ground cinnamon
½ cup chopped walnuts
½ teaspoon ground allspice
½ teaspoon grated nutmeg
½ cup dried currants
½ cup extra-virgin olive oil

Soak bread crumbs in milk until softened, then combine with other ingredients except olive oil and mix well. Shape mixture into walnut-size balls. Heat oil in a skillet, then fry meatballs in several batches until browned. Drain on paper towels and serve while still warm. *Serves 6 to 8.*

*Ellen Rievman
is a dancer in the Metropolitan
Opera Ballet.*

Harold H. Healy, Jr.
Quiche à l'Oignon

2 cups diced onions
3 tablespoons butter
3 eggs, lightly beaten
3 tablespoons flour
1 cup light cream or half-and-half
½ teaspoon salt
Black pepper to taste
1 unbaked 9-inch pie shell
Grated nutmeg

Preheat oven to 400 degrees. In a skillet, sauté onions in butter until transparent; do not let brown. In a bowl, blend eggs, flour, and cream. Season with salt and pepper. Cover the bottom of the pie shell with the sautéed onions, then pour in the egg mixture. Sprinkle grated nutmeg on top. Bake until delicately browned and well set, about 35 minutes. *Serves 4 to 6.*

Note If using a frozen pie shell, defrost it for 10 minutes before using.

Harold H. Healy, Jr.
is the Treasurer of the Metropolitan
Opera Guild, and an Advisory
Director of the Metropolitan Opera
Association. This recipe is from his
wife, Elizabeth Healy.

Marilyn Horne
Spanakopeta
SPINACH PIE APPETIZER

2½ cups flour
¾ cup olive oil
Pinch each of salt and pepper
3 bunches fresh spinach (about 2 pounds),
   cleaned, stems removed
1 medium onion or 1 bunch scallions, finely
   chopped
½ pound feta cheese, coarsely crumbled
1 teaspoon chopped fresh dill
1 egg, well beaten
2 teaspoons sesame seed

Marilyn Horne serves up pasta for Paolo Montarsolo in
L'Italiana in Algeri.

Amelita Galli-Curci (right) with friends at the Chicago Horse Show.

Preheat oven to 350 degrees. Place flour in a medium bowl. Add ¼ cup olive oil, a pinch of salt, and enough water (about ¼ cup) to make a medium-firm dough. Briefly knead the dough, then shape into 2 equal balls. Roll 1 ball out until about ⅛-inch thick and about 10 × 14 inches. Grease a 9 × 13-inch baking pan, then place dough in the pan, fitting it into the edges.

Chop spinach well. Place in a large bowl, and add the onion or scallions, feta, remaining olive oil, pepper, and dill. Mix well and pour mixture in the baking pan. Roll out top sheet of dough and put on top. With a knife, lightly score squares on the dough. Brush top with beaten egg and sprinkle with sesame seed. Bake for 1 to 1½ hours, depending on how crunchy you like the finished product. Let sit for a few minutes, then cut into squares and serve. *Serves 12.*

Marilyn Horne
is one of today's most celebrated
singers. In 1970 she made her Met
debut as Adalgisa in Norma, *and*
since then has returned to delight
audiences in such roles as Carmen,
Isabella in L'Italiana in Algeri, *and Rosina in* Il Barbiere di Siviglia. *She makes her home in New York City.*

Millicent Hacker
Baked Clams

1 (16-ounce) can minced clams, including liquid
½ cup (1 stick) butter, melted
1 small onion, grated
½ cup grated Parmesan cheese
½ teaspoon crushed garlic
1 teaspoon dried oregano
25 Ritz crackers, crushed

Preheat oven to 350 degrees. In a bowl, mix ingredients, then put mixture in a 9-inch baking dish and bake until golden brown and bubbly, about 25 minutes. Serve at once. *Serves 6.*

Note If desired, spoon mixture into clamshell halves and place stuffed shells in a large baking dish or on a baking sheet. Bake until tops are lightly browned, about 15 minutes.

*Millicent Hacker
is the Wardrobe Supervisor at the
Metropolitan Opera.*

OPPOSITE: *Astrid Varnay inspects operatic party napkins.*

Lenore Rosenberg
Ekstrom's Julglögg

½ gallon Port wine
1 quart vodka or a fifth of whiskey
1 cup water
½–⅔ cup sugar
½ cup raisins
¼ cup blanched almonds, whole or sliced
1 half-inch cinnamon stick
5 whole cloves
Seeds from 1 cardamom pod
2–3 slivers orange peel

In a large pot with a tight-fitting cover, mix wine and vodka. In a small saucepan, heat water, add sugar, and stir until dissolved. Add sugar mixture to the wine and vodka, along with remaining ingredients. Cover and bring to a simmer; do not let boil. Remove cover, ignite, and immediately replace cover to put out the flame. *Be careful!* Repeat this twice more, stirring the mixture between each flaming. Serve warm. *Makes about 3 quarts.*

Note For a nonalcoholic alternative, use the same spices in hot cider.

*Lenore Rosenberg
is an Administrative Assistant in the
Artistic Department of the Met.*

Thomas J. Hubbard
Cocktail de Lady Charles
COURTESY LE VICOMTE DE
NOAILLES

Recette pour une dizaine de verres à cocktail:

Dans une grande carafe,
  Verser un petit verre de COGNAC
  Ajouter une grande cuillerée à soupe de
    SUCRE
  Ajouter 15 gouttes de ANGUSTURA
    Bitters et
6 rondelles de CITRON
Laisser reposer pendant une heure
Mélanger
Ajouter beaucoup de glace
Puis une petite bouteille de PERRIER et une
bouteille de CHAMPAGNE

Préparation a faire une heure avant de servir.

To a large carafe, add a small glass of cognac, a heaping tablespoon of sugar, 15 drops Angustura Bitters, and 6 slices of lemon. Let stand for 1 hour.

Mix well, then add lots of ice, a small bottle of Perrier, and a bottle of Champagne.

Prepare the cocktail 1 hour before serving. *Serves 4 to 6.*

Thomas J. Hubbard
is Chairman of the Board of the
Metropolitan Opera Guild, and an
Advisory Director of the Metro-
politan Opera Association.

Metropolitan Opera Club

❧ ❧

WINE LIST

❧ ❧

VINTAGE CHAMPAGNES
IMPORTED FROM LONDON

	QTS.	PTS.
Clicquot '98	$4.00	$2.25
Krug '98	4.00	2.25
Pol Roger '98	4.00	2.25

LIQUORS

PER DRINK	PER DRINK
RYE WHISKEY,	**IRISH WHISKEY,**
Pasque Island....15c	"V. O. P.".....20c
Hannisville....15c	Old Tom Gin....15c
Mt. Vernon, 1887....25c	Plymouth Gin....15c
SCOTCH WHISKEY,	Holland Gin....15c
"Clubland,"Morten&Co20c	Old Cognac, Pony, 15c, 25c
Jopp's Highland....20c	Cognac, Vierge 1868,
	Pony, 25c, 35c

WINES

PER GLASS	PER GLASS
Claret, St. Estephe....15c	Sherry, Montilla F.,

LIQUEURS

Creme de Menthe,Green.20c	Yellow Chartreuse.....20c
Benedictine....20c	Absinthe....20c
Curacao....20c	Italian Vermouth....20c
Maraschino....20c	French Vermouth....20c

MISCELLANEOUS

PER BOTTLE	PER BOTTLE
Bass Ale, White Label..30c	Ginger Ale, Imported..20c
Stout, Guinness'....30c	Seltzer or Carbonic per
	glass....10c
Imperial Beer, Beadleston & Woerz, 15c	

MINERAL WATERS

	QTS.	PTS.
Apollinaris	35c	20c
Londonderry Lithia	35c	20c

CIGARS
MORTEN & CO.
Made to Order of Special Weights

Cabanas Regalia, Excelente	25c
Pedro Murias, Murias	22c
Bock, Chicquitos	15c
Rosa Rositas	15c

CIGARETTES
Per Box of 10

Beverly Sills in Don Pasquale.
OPPOSITE: *Opera Club wine list, 1905.*

Aage Haugland
The Ho-jo-to-ho Cure

OR

"HOW-TO-KILL-A-COLD-
ON-A-ROCK-THE-NIGHT-
BEFORE"

1 bottle strong Danish export beer (of course!)
5 cloves of garlic, crushed
1 egg yolk
1 small (but not too small) glass Danish export
schnapps (of course!)
5 chlorophyll tablets

Heat beer almost to the boiling point, and add garlic, egg yolk, and schnapps. Mix, then drink as hot as possible together with chlorophyll tablets, preferably in bed (alone?). *Serves 1.*

Aage Haugland
was born in Copenhagen, and sang at Covent Garden, La Scala, Salzburg, and Bayreuth before coming to the Met in 1979. Since then he has performed many important bass roles with the company. He writes, "This is a recipe I composed in Salzburg some years ago when I got a sore throat the day before an opening night. My family didn't believe their eyes—or their noses—but the next morning found me as healthy as ever."

Broiled Curried Eggs
Mrs. John Barry Ryan

Oyster Omelet Jenny Lind

Gombás Velö Tojással
Eva Marton

Fonduta
Fiorenza Cossotto

Sour Cream and Chive Soufflé
Oscar de la Renta

Mexican Vegetable Sauce
Linore Aronson

Bananas Erna Berger
Erna Berger

Endive Pelletier
Rose Bampton

Lattuga à la Caruso

Pasta with Cheese Buongusto
David Hamilton

Charlotte d'Aubergines
Joan Sutherland

Koosa
Herb Wekselblatt

Zucchini "Lasagna"
Wendy Westwood

Stuffed Eggplant Casserole
Leontyne Price

"The Shell Game"
Eleanor Steber

OPPOSITE: *Eleanor Steber.* OVERLEAF: *Joan Sutherland's Charlotte d'Aubergines, and the dagger she used in* Lucia di Lammermoor. *Dame Joan is shown as Marie.*

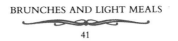
BRUNCHES AND LIGHT MEALS

Mrs. John Barry Ryan
Broiled Curried Eggs

6 hard-boiled eggs
2 tablespoons mayonnaise
Salt and pepper to taste
1½ cups chicken broth
3 tablespoons flour
1 teaspoon curry powder
Fine dry bread crumbs

Cut eggs in half lengthwise, remove yolks, and run yolks through a fine sieve. Combine yolks with the mayonnaise and season with salt and pepper. Blend the mixture until smooth, then fill the egg-white halves with the yolk mixture.

In a small saucepan, heat the chicken broth, blend in the flour and curry powder, and stir until smooth and thickened. Put each stuffed egg half in a 1-cup ramekin, cover with the curry sauce, and sprinkle with bread crumbs. Place under a broiler for a few minutes, until piping hot and lightly browned. This is a nice first course for lunch. *Serves 6.*

Mrs. John Barry Ryan
is an Honorary Director of the
Metropolitan Opera Association.
Her father, the late Otto Kahn, was
for many years President of the Met.

Oyster Omelet Jenny Lind

6 large oysters, shucked, liquor reserved
4 eggs, separated
1 tablespoon light cream
Pinch of cayenne pepper
Salt and pepper to taste
2 tablespoons (¼ stick) butter

Poach oysters in their liquor until the edges start to curl, about 3 minutes. Drain well and cut into pieces. Combine egg yolks, cream, and cayenne, then season with salt and pepper. Beat the mixture lightly with a fork. Blend in oysters. Stiffly beat the egg whites, then fold into oyster mixture.

In an omelet pan, heat butter, pour in the egg mixture, and stir gently with a fork. When the eggs start to set, fold omelet in half. Cook for another minute, then slide onto a plate and serve. *Serves 2.*

Oyster Omelet Jenny Lind
was a nineteenth-century tribute to
Jenny Lind (1820–1887), hailed as
"the Swedish Nightingale." She re-
tired the year the Met opened and
never sang with the company. Miss
Lind was a favored guest at
Delmonico's when the hotel and
restaurant was downtown on Broad-
way, not far from Bowling Green.

OPPOSITE: *Jenny Lind.*

Eva Marton
Gombás Velö Tojással
CALVES BRAINS,
MUSHROOMS, AND
SCRAMBLED EGGS ON
TOAST

1 pound calves brains
1 tablespoon bacon drippings or butter
1 medium onion, finely chopped
⅓ cup chopped fresh chives
½ cup sliced fresh mushrooms
½ teaspoon paprika
Salt to taste
Freshly ground white pepper to taste
3 eggs
1 tablespoon heavy cream
Toasted slices of rye bread
Grated Parmesan cheese (optional)

Soak brains in cold water for 2 hours, then carefully remove membranes. Pat brains dry and chop finely. In a skillet, heat bacon fat, then add onion and chives. Cover and cook over very low heat until onion is transparent, about 10 minutes. Do not let brown.

Add brains, mushrooms, paprika, and salt and white pepper; mix gently, cover, and cook over low heat for about 10 minutes. Stir a couple of times to prevent scorching or drying out.

Beat eggs with a pinch of salt and the cream; add to the mixture. Raise heat to high, and stir continually to scramble the mixture, but make sure that it doesn't get hard and dry out—it should remain quite creamy. Correct seasoning, then serve over rye toast or serve toast separately. Grated Parmesan can be served on the side; although this is not a Hungarian tradition, it is an interesting variation on the theme. *Serves 4.*

Note This mixture can be used as a filling for savory crepes, called *palacsinta* by Hungarians.

Eva Marton
is one of today's most celebrated sopranos, well known for her portrayals of Turandot, Tosca, and other roles. She and her family live in Hamburg. She notes that, "According to a whimsical Hungarian folk story, when a child is born the parents put a book of poetry, a cooking spoon, and sheet music in the crib, and if the baby reaches toward the poems he or she will be a poet. The sheet music clearly indicates a musical career and, naturally, the spoon heralds a cook. I must have been interested in the second and third objects, because my life is strongly influenced by both."

OPPOSITE: *Plácido Domingo and Eva Marton.*

Fiorenza Cossotto
Fonduta

1 pound Italian fontina cheese, cut into small
chunks
1 teaspoon cornstarch, dissolved in ½ cup milk
¼ teaspoon salt
⅛ teaspoon white pepper
3 egg yolks
12 toasted, buttered triangles of French bread
1 (2-ounce) can white truffles, sliced

In a 2-quart saucepan, put cheese and cornstarch-milk mixture; season with salt and white pepper. Cook over low heat, stirring constantly, for about 5 minutes, or until cheese melts. Beat yolks lightly for a few seconds, then spoon about ¼ cup of the cheese mixture into the yolks and beat vigorously. Pour the mixture slowly back into the pan, still beating, and continue cooking the cheese mixture over low heat until it becomes smooth and finally begins to thicken to a heavy cream, about 2 minutes. Ladle it immediately into heated soup bowls. Arrange truffle slices on top and toast triangles around the inside edges of bowls. *Serves 4.*

Fiorenza Cossotto
made her Met debut in 1968, and
continues to sing important mezzo
roles with the company.

Oscar de la Renta
Sour Cream and Chive Soufflé

½ cup freshly grated Parmesan cheese
1¼ cups sour cream
½ cup sifted flour
5 eggs, separated, plus 2 extra egg whites
½ cup finely chopped fresh chives
1 teaspoon salt, or to taste
Freshly ground black pepper to taste

Preheat oven to 350 degrees. Butter the inside of a 2-quart soufflé dish, then coat with a little grated Parmesan; shake off any excess cheese and chill the dish.

Put sour cream in a bowl, sift flour into it, and whip with a wire whisk until well blended. Continue whisking and add egg yolks, one by one. Stir in chives, salt and pepper, and remaining cheese. Beat egg whites until they form peaks and fold them carefully into the mixture. Pour into the soufflé dish and bake until puffy and lightly browned, about 30 to 35 minutes. *Serves 4.*

Oscar de la Renta
the well-known fashion designer, is a
member of the Board of Directors of
the Metropolitan Opera Guild, and
a Member of the Metropolitan
Opera Association.

Linore Aronson
Mexican Vegetable Sauce

1 medium onion, chopped

1 carrot, peeled, halved, then sliced

1 celery stalk, chopped

6 scallions (green part included), chopped; plus
    additional for garnish

1 clove garlic, pressed

1 zucchini, chopped

1½ cups corn kernels, fresh or thawed

2 cups cooked pinto beans

¼ cup chopped green chilies

1 tablespoon chili powder

1 tablespoon dried oregano

Salt to taste

⅛ teaspoon cayenne pepper

½ cup water

Chopped ripe tomatoes, shredded lettuce, bean
    sprouts for garnish

Simmer the first 6 ingredients in ½ cup of water for 10 minutes. Add remaining ingredients, mix well, cover, and cook over medium-low heat for 20 minutes. Stir occasionally and add a little more water if needed.

Serve over brown rice or use to fill pita bread. Garnish with tomatoes, additional chopped scallions, shredded lettuce, and sprouts. *Makes about 1 quart.*

Linore Aronson
is a soprano in the Metropolitan
Opera Chorus.

Erna Berger
Bananas Erna Berger

2 tablespoons (¼ stick) butter

4 ripe bananas

Curry powder to taste

4 thin slices boiled or baked ham

2 tablespoons sliced blanched almonds

Cooked white rice

In a skillet, heat butter and sauté bananas over medium-high heat, turning them carefully until lightly browned. Remove to a warm plate and sprinkle with curry powder. In the same skillet, sauté ham slices for a minute or so. Wrap each banana in a ham slice, and place on serving dish. Sauté almonds quickly to toast them, then sprinkle over bananas. Serve with rice. *Serves 4.*

Erna Berger
sang leading soprano roles internationally for many years, and is
particularly remembered for her Met
performances as Sophie in Der
Rosenkavalier. *She now lives in*
Essen. "I am glad to send you a
little recipe which I like very much
for a snack or a light lunch."

Rose Bampton
Endive Pelletier

12 medium Belgian endive
Salt
1 cup heavy cream
½ cup (1 stick) butter, in pieces
1½ cups grated Emmental (Swiss) cheese
Black pepper to taste

Wash and dry endive, discard any discolored outer leaves, and trim the bases. Tie the endives in small bundles to keep their shape while cooking. Blanch in lightly salted boiling water for about 15 minutes. Drain well.

Preheat oven to 350 degrees. Butter a large casserole. Place the endives in the casserole, season with salt and pepper, and pour the cream over. Top with pats of butter and sprinkle with grated cheese. Bake for about 20 minutes, then place under the broiler to quickly brown the top. *Serves 4.*

*Rose Bampton
made her Met debut in 1932, and for
seventeen seasons sang both soprano
and mezzo roles for the company,
and is a Member of the Metropolitan
Opera Association. Since retiring
she has taught in New York and
Montreal. This dish is named for
her late husband, the conductor
Wilfrid Pelletier.*

Lattuga à la Caruso

2 heads very firm iceberg lettuce
1 tablespoon butter, in pieces
½ cup white bread crumbs mixed with 2
    tablespoons melted butter
2 tablespoons grated Parmesan cheese
Salt and pepper to taste

Preheat oven to 400 degrees. Butter a shallow casserole dish. Cut lettuce in quarters, leaving core in. Boil in salted water for 5 minutes, then drain and arrange in casserole dish. Dot with butter. Mix buttered crumbs with the cheese and salt and pepper. Sprinkle over dish and bake until brown, about 15 minutes. *Serves 8.*

*Lattuga à la Caruso
was named after Enrico Caruso
(1873–1921), the legendary tenor
who was probably the most famous
opera singer of all time. He sang at
the Met for eighteen seasons, a total
of 626 performances, and his recordings continue to delight opera lovers.
This dish was first prepared and
named by the chef of New York's old
Knickerbocker Hotel, where Caruso
often stayed. The tenor was said to
have been particularly fond of it,
especially on days when he had to
sing, as it is so light.*

OPPOSITE: *Victoria de los Angeles.*

David Hamilton
Pasta with Cheese Buongusto

1 (12-ounce) box spiral pasta (rotelle)
5 tablespoons butter
1 small onion, diced
¼ cup flour
2½ cups milk
¼ teaspoon grated nutmeg
Salt and pepper to taste
8 ounces cheddar cheese, thinly sliced
8 ounces Monterey Jack or muenster cheese,
    thinly sliced

Preheat oven to 375 degrees. Cook pasta in lightly salted water until barely *al dente*. Do not over-cook! In a skillet, sauté onion in 1 tablespoon butter until translucent; do not brown. Melt remaining butter in a saucepan, remove from heat, then stir in flour and blend until smooth. Return to medium heat and slowly add 1 cup of the milk, stirring until smooth and thickened, about 2 minutes. Add another cup of milk, the sautéed onion, and the nutmeg and salt and pepper. Stir constantly until smooth and thickened, then add remaining milk. Reduce heat and stir for another minute.

Cover the bottom of a large casserole with a small amount of the sauce, cover with a layer of pasta, then follow with a layer of mixed sliced cheeses and more sauce. Continue with layers and finish with a topping of sauce. Push remaining slices of cheese down the sides of the casserole. Bake until bubbling and cheese melts, about 10 to 15 minutes. *Serves 4.*

David Hamilton
made his Met debut in 1986, and
has sung baritone roles in
Rigoletto, Carmen, Manon, *and*
Dialogues of the Carmelites. *He*
adds, "No one will ever kid you
about eating macaroni and cheese
after they taste this!"

Blanche Thebom.

Joan Sutherland
Charlotte d'Aubergines
EGGPLANT CHARLOTTE

3–4 small eggplants (about 1¾ pounds)
Salt
½ cup olive oil
1 medium onion, minced
1 clove garlic, crushed
10 ripe medium tomatoes, peeled, seeded, and
  chopped; or 2 pounds canned plum tomatoes,
  drained
Freshly ground black pepper
8 ounces plain yogurt
½ cup beef broth

Wipe the eggplants, trim the stem ends, and cut into ¾-inch lengthwise slices. Put the slices on a flat surface, sprinkle with salt, and let stand for 30 minutes. Rinse the slices with cold water and dry on paper towels.

In a saucepan, heat 2 tablespoons oil and sauté onion until light brown. Add garlic and tomatoes, season with salt and pepper, and cook, stirring occasionally, until the mixture is thick and pulpy, about 20 to 25 minutes. Heat the remaining oil in a skillet and sauté the eggplant slices to brown on both sides.

Preheat oven to 350 degrees. Arrange a layer of overlapping eggplant slices in a greased 2-quart charlotte mold or cake pan. Reserve one-third of the tomato mixture. Spread the layer of eggplant with some of the remaining tomato mixture, then top with yogurt. Continue the layers, finishing with eggplant. Combine the reserved tomato mixture with the broth in a saucepan, heat, and stir until smooth to make a sauce.

Cover the mold with foil and bake for 40 to 45 minutes. Cool a little, then unmold onto a serving dish. Correct seasoning of the tomato sauce and spoon over the eggplant. *Serves 4.*

Joan Sutherland
has had one of the most remarkable
singing careers of this century. Born
in Sydney, Australia, she has been
an international star for the last
twenty-eight years. After her Met
debut in 1961, she returned more
than 200 times to thrill audiences in
such roles as Lucia, Violetta,
Norma, Gilda, and Donna Anna.
Dame Joan and her husband, con-
ductor Richard Bonynge, live in
Switzerland.

OVERLEAF: *Sherrill Milnes and Renata Scotto in the*
Banquet Scene from Macbeth.

Herb Wekselblatt
Koosa

STUFFED ZUCCHINI

2 pounds boneless lamb shoulder, coarsely ground
1 cup white rice
Salt and pepper to taste
Small pinch of ground cinnamon
12 small zucchini (about 6 pounds)
½ cup water
½ teaspoon dried mint, crushed
1 (12-ounce) can tomato sauce, diluted with 1 cup
    water

Mix meat, rice, salt and pepper, and cinnamon; set aside. Wash zucchini and hollow out, leaving a shell about ⅓ inch thick. Stuff zucchini shells with meat mixture until no more than two-thirds full, since rice will expand during cooking.

In a small bowl, combine water, mint, and a small pinch of salt. Roll each stuffed zucchini in this mixture. Place stuffed zucchini in a large skillet or heatproof baking pan, then cover with the diluted tomato sauce. Cover pan and cook over low heat for 1 hour, or bake at 375 degrees for 1¼ to 1½ hours. *Serves 6.*

*Herb Wekselblatt
is the tuba player in the Metropolitan Opera Orchestra.*

Wendy Westwood
Zucchini "Lasagna"

1 tablespoon butter
½ pound fresh mushrooms, thinly sliced
3 large zucchini (about 2¼ pounds)
⅓ cup flour
Salt and pepper to taste
Oil for frying (about ¼ cup)
1 (15-ounce) container part-skim ricotta cheese
2 eggs
1 cup chopped Italian (flat) parsley
1 teaspoon dried basil
⅓ cup grated Parmesan cheese
2 cups marinara sauce
½ pound part-skim mozzarella cheese, grated

Preheat oven to 400 degrees. In a large skillet, heat butter and sauté mushrooms until soft; set them aside. Cut zucchini lengthwise into ¼-inch-thick slices. Season flour with salt and pepper, then dust both sides of zucchini with flour. In a skillet, heat oil and sauté zucchini over medium heat until golden, turning them once. Set slices on paper towels to drain. In a bowl, combine ricotta, eggs, parsley, basil, and ¼ cup Parmesan.

Spread 1 cup of marinara sauce in the bottom of a 12 × 8 × 2-inch baking pan, top with half the zucchini slices, then spread with half of the ricotta mixture, half the mushrooms, and half the mozzarella. Repeat the layers. Sprinkle top with remaining Parmesan.

Bake until bubbly, about 25 minutes. Let stand for about 10 minutes before serving. *Serves 4 to 6*.

*Wendy Westwood
is the Assistant Director of Development of the Metropolitan Opera.*

Lawrence Tibbett.

Leontyne Price
Stuffed Eggplant Casserole

1 large eggplant (about 1¼ pounds)
2 tablespoons (¼ stick) butter
1 cup chopped onions
1 cup chopped fresh mushrooms
1 heaping teaspoon dried basil or oregano
1 teaspoon salt
¼ teaspoon freshly ground black pepper
1 cup cooked ground beef
½ cup dry bread crumbs
Minced fresh parsley or grated Parmesan cheese

Preheat oven to 350 degrees. Wrap eggplant in aluminum foil and bake until soft, about 50 minutes. Cool the eggplant, then cut it in half lengthwise. Scoop out pulp, leaving ½-inch-thick shells. Chop the pulp.

In a skillet, heat butter and add onions, mushrooms, herbs, and seasonings. Sauté until onions and mushrooms are soft. Add mixture to the chopped eggplant pulp, then stir in the ground beef and bread crumbs. Mix well, and correct seasoning. Fill the shells with the mixture, then place the shells in a casserole or baking dish just large enough to hold them. Bake until hot, about 15 minutes. Sprinkle with minced parsley or grated Parmesan and serve. *Serves 2 to 4.*

Leontyne Price
was born in Laurel, Mississippi,
and sang in San Francisco, Verona,
Vienna, London, and Milan before
her triumphant Met debut in 1961.
She has sung sixteen roles at the
Met, including Cleopatra on the
opening night of the new Metro-
politan Opera House, and is one of
the best-known operatic artists sing-
ing today. Now retired from the
opera stage, she still sings many
concerts and recitals.

Eleanor Steber.

Christa Ludwig and Walter Berry in Der Rosenkavalier.

Eleanor Steber
"The Shell Game"

2 large onions, thinly sliced
2 tablespoons (¼ stick) butter
2 cloves garlic, chopped
1½ pounds ground beef
1 (16-ounce) can tomato sauce
2 (6-ounce) cans pitted black olives, halved or
  quartered
2 tablespoons chili powder
1 (1-pound) box pasta shells
1 pound sharp cheddar cheese, grated

Preheat oven to 350 degrees. In a skillet, sauté onions in butter until soft and lightly browned. Add garlic and meat, then sauté to brown the meat. Remove from heat. Blend the mixture with tomato sauce, olives, and chili powder; set aside. Cook shells in boiling water until just done (*al dente*).

In a large baking dish, put a layer of shells, then a layer of beef sauce, and cover with a layer of grated cheese. Continue with alternating layers, finishing with grated cheese. Bake until hot and bubbly, about 45 minutes. Serve with green salad and garlic bread. *Serves 6.*

Eleanor Steber
first sang at the Met in 1940, and
thereafter gave the company twenty-
two seasons of glorious singing. Best
known for her performances of the
Mozart soprano roles, she also sang
Verdi, Strauss, and even some
Wagner and Berg, and created the
title role in Barber's Vanessa. *Since*
her retirement she has taught sing-
ing. She lives in New York City.

Pumpkin Soup
Thomas Lucia

Spinach Soup
Alton E. Peters

Consommé Rossini

Chłodnick
Teresa Kubiak

Curried Zucchini Soup
Bidú Sayão

Hungarian Goulash Soup
Sherrill Milnes

Tomato Soup
Leonie Rysanek

Kraasesuppe mit Melboeller
Lauritz Melchior

Leek and Watercress Soup
Bruce Crawford

Soupe à Sara
Frederica von Stade

OVERLEAF: *Sherrill Milnes's Hungarian Goulash Soup, and the jester's stick he used in* Rigoletto. *Mr. Milnes is shown as Iago.*

SOUPS

Thomas Lucia
Pumpkin Soup

¼ cup (½ stick) butter
4 cups chopped fresh pumpkin or winter squash
2 large yellow onions, chopped (about 1½ cups)
6 cups canned or homemade chicken broth
2 celery stalks, chopped
2 medium potatoes, peeled and diced
1 teaspoon paprika
1–2 tablespoons fresh lemon juice
¼ teaspoon Tabasco, or to taste
Salt to taste
1 cup heavy cream

In a saucepan, heat butter and add pumpkin and onions. Sauté over low heat for 6 to 8 minutes, stirring a few times; do not let brown. Slowly add broth, then add the celery, potatoes, paprika, lemon juice, Tabasco, and salt. Bring to a boil, reduce heat, cover, and simmer for 30 minutes.

Push mixture through a food mill to strain well, and discard any pulp. Stir in cream, blend well, and serve. If prepared in advance, do not let soup come to a boil when reheating. This soup can be served cold as well. *Serves 6 to 8.*

*Thomas Lucia
was the Manager of Donor Services
in the Met's Development Department.*

Alton E. Peters
Spinach Soup

1½ tablespoons butter
1 small onion, chopped
1½ tablespoons flour
4 cups canned chicken broth
1 clove garlic, slivered
1 (10-ounce) package frozen chopped spinach
2 egg yolks
Pinch of grated nutmeg
Salt and pepper to taste
1 cup heavy cream

In a saucepan, heat butter and sauté onion until transparent, about 5 minutes; do not brown. Add flour, stir and blend, then gradually add the chicken broth, stirring until smooth. Add garlic, cover the pan, and simmer for 10 minutes. Add spinach and simmer until defrosted and cooked, about 5 minutes.

Put egg yolks in a blender or processor bowl, add a little of the hot soup, and blend for a few seconds. Gradually add all of the soup and blend well. Return mixture to the saucepan. Season with nutmeg and salt and pepper, then add cream and mix well. Reheat gently for serving, but do not let the soup boil. *Serves 6.*

*Alton E. Peters
is President of the Metropolitan
Opera Guild, and a Vice-President
of the Metropolitan Opera Association. This is a favorite family recipe
from his wife, Elizabeth Peters.*

Consommé Rossini

*6 cups chicken consommé or strong chicken broth
1½ tablespoons quick-cooking tapioca
¼ cup black truffles
½ cup pâté de foie gras
12 small cream puffs or rounds of white toast*

Place consommé and tapioca in a saucepan. Bring to a boil, then lower heat and simmer for 5 minutes.

In a blender or processor, puree the truffles, add the pâté, and process until smooth. Fill the cream puffs with the mixture or spread on toast rounds; serve with the consommé. *Serves 4 to 6.*

*Consommé Rossini
was named after Gioachino Rossini
(1792–1868). The great composer of
Il Barbiere di Siviglia, Guillaume
Tell, and many other operas was
also a great gourmet, and once wrote
that "the stomach is the conductor
who leads the great orchestra of our
passions." Many recipes were named
after him; the best known is Tournedos Rossini, but in addition to the
above consommé there are also Tim-
bales Rossini, Eggs Rossini,
Chicken Rossini, and Sweetbreads
Rossini. He was especially fond of
pâté de foie gras and truffles, and
most preparations bearing his name
include one or both of these delicacies.*

Gioachino Rossini.

Teresa Kubiak
Chłodnik

1 pound boneless veal, trimmed and cubed

1 carrot, peeled and sliced

1 parsnip, peeled and sliced

1 leek (white part only), washed, trimmed, and
   sliced

1 pound young beets, peeled

1 cup sour cream

2 hard-boiled eggs, chopped

2 cucumbers, peeled, seeded, and chopped

8 medium shrimp, cooked, peeled, and minced

1 tablespoon minced fresh dill

1 tablespoon minced scallions

Pinch of sugar

1 tablespoon distilled white vinegar

2 small dill pickles, minced

2 cups buttermilk

Salt and pepper to taste

In a saucepan, place veal, carrot, parsnip, and leek. Cover with water, put on lid, and cook over medium heat for 20 minutes. Drain, discard vegetables, and mince meat. Cook beets with water to cover until tender, then drain and mince. Combine minced meat and beets with remaining ingredients and refrigerate. When ready to serve, allow chłodnik to come close to room temperature; it should be cool, not cold. *Serves 4 to 6.*

*Teresa Kubiak
was born in Lodz, Poland, and first
came to the Met in 1973, later
singing fourteen leading soprano
roles. "My favorite summer dish at
home is Chłodnik, a wonderfully
refreshing cold soup that's a whole
meal in itself. It's the only dish I
would cherish on even the hottest
days of summer."*

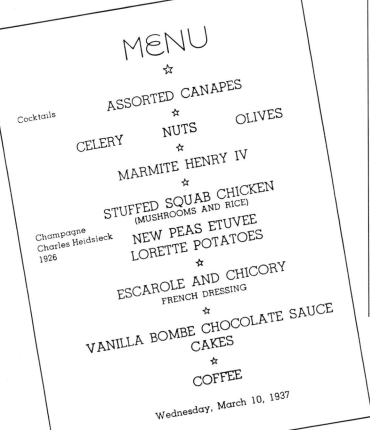

MENU

☆

ASSORTED CANAPES

☆

Cocktails

CELERY   NUTS   OLIVES

☆

MARMITE HENRY IV

☆

STUFFED SQUAB CHICKEN
(MUSHROOMS AND RICE)

Champagne
Charles Heidsieck
1926

NEW PEAS ETUVEE
LORETTE POTATOES

☆

ESCAROLE AND CHICORY
FRENCH DRESSING

☆

VANILLA BOMBE CHOCOLATE SAUCE
CAKES

☆

COFFEE

Wednesday, March 10, 1937

LEFT: *A 1937 Opera Club menu.* OPPOSITE: *Teresa Kubiak.*

Bidú Sayão
Curried Zucchini Soup

2 medium zucchini (about 1½ pounds)
2 tablespoons (¼ stick) butter
1 teaspoon curry powder, or to taste
2 cups chicken broth
1 small red onion, very finely diced
Salt and pepper to taste
1 cup plain yogurt or heavy cream
Minced fresh parsley

Trim and wash zucchini, then slice about ¾ inch thick. In a heavy saucepan or skillet, heat butter, add zucchini, cover tightly, and cook over low heat until zucchini are soft, about 10 minutes; do not let brown. Sprinkle zucchini with curry powder, mix well, then pour contents of pan, including pan juices, into the bowl of a food processor or blender. Add broth and process until smooth. Pour into a bowl, stir in diced onion, and season with salt and pepper. Chill. *Serves 4.*

To serve the soup cold, add ½ cup yogurt to the chilled soup and whisk until well blended. Ladle into serving bowls or cups, sprinkle with parsley, and pass a small bowl with the remaining yogurt for putting a dollop on each serving.

To serve the soup hot, it is best made the day before and chilled overnight. Before serving, heat to a simmer and then stir in ½ cup of heavy cream. Whip remaining cream and pass with the soup. This soup is delicious hot.

To freeze the soup, it is best made when zucchini are fresh, young, and tender. This soup freezes beautifully and may be kept for up to a year in the freezer. Follow the above recipe, but add only 1 cup of broth and no cream or yogurt. When ready to serve, defrost, add second cup of broth, and bring to a simmer. Then proceed as above, adding either yogurt to cold soup or cream to hot soup.

*Bidú Sayão
was born in Rio de Janeiro, and came to the Met in 1937, following important engagements in Europe and South America. She sang leading soprano roles with the company for sixteen seasons, and is fondly remembered by many for her portrayals of Juliette, Mimi, Susanna, Norina, and many others. She retired from singing in 1957, and now lives at her Casa Bidú in Maine. She is a Member of the Metropolitan Opera Association.*

OPPOSITE: *Bidú Sayão.*

Sherrill Milnes
Hungarian Goulash Soup

¼ cup (½ stick) butter

1½ pounds boneless beef chuck or round, cubed

6 cups canned beef broth

2 large onions, coarsely chopped

1½ tablespoons Hungarian sweet paprika

1 teaspoon dried marjoram (optional)

1 teaspoon caraway seed

½ pound spicy sausage (kielbasa or other), thickly sliced

1 (1-pound) can peeled tomatoes, chopped with juice

1 tablespoon dark brown sugar

½ small head green cabbage, coarsely chopped

2 large potatoes (about 1 pound), peeled and cubed

Salt and pepper to taste

In a large, heavy skillet, heat 1½ tablespoons butter and brown the beef cubes. Transfer the browned beef to a heavy kettle or large saucepan. Deglaze the skillet with a little of the broth and add cooking liquid to the beef.

Heat the remaining butter in the same skillet, and sauté the onions until soft and light yellow, about 5 minutes; add the paprika, marjoram, and caraway seed; blend well, then add the mixture to the beef along with the sausage, tomatoes and juice, brown sugar, and remaining beef broth. Bring to a boil, then reduce heat, cover, and cook over low heat for about 1 hour. Add cabbage and potatoes, season with salt and pepper, and cook until beef and potatoes are tender, about another 45 minutes. *Serves 6.*

Sherrill Milnes hails from Downers Grove, Illinois. After engagements in Santa Fe and Baltimore and with the New York City Opera, he made his Met debut in 1965, and has been a mainstay of the company ever since, singing more than 375 performances of thirty roles. He has also had an extensive international career, and can be heard on many recordings.

Leonie Rysanek
Tomato Soup

3 pounds ripe tomatoes
2 quarts water, approximately
Salt and pepper to taste
Pinch of sugar
½ cup heavy cream, whipped
3 tablespoons finely minced ham

Use only the best tomatoes. Cut them into large cubes and place in a kettle with water barely to cover. Add salt and pepper and the sugar. Bring to a boil, cover, and simmer over low heat until tomatoes are done; depending on ripeness, this may take 1 to 3 hours. Strain soup, which should have some body. Correct seasoning and serve garnished with whipped cream and a sprinkling of minced ham. *Serves 4 to 6.*

Leonie Rysanek
was born in Vienna, and sang there
as well as at La Scala, Paris,
Bayreuth, and San Francisco before
making her Met debut in 1959 as the
company's first Lady Macbeth.
Since then she has returned nearly
every season, singing more than 230
performances of twenty roles. In
1984 the Met staged a gala to
celebrate her twenty-fifth anniver-
sary with the company.

Leonie Rysanek.
OPPOSITE: *From a 1917 Met program.*

Lauritz Melchior
Kraasesuppe mit Melboeller
GIBLET SOUP WITH FLOUR DUMPLINGS

Soup

½ pound chicken, goose, or duck giblets

Salt and pepper to taste

3 tart apples, sliced

4 pitted prunes, soaked in hot water for 30 minutes

2 carrots, thinly sliced

1 celery stalk, diced

2 leeks (white part only) or 1 onion, chopped

1 teaspoon sugar

1 tablespoon distilled white vinegar

Dumplings

¼ cup (½ stick) butter

¾ cup flour

1 cup water, approximately

2 eggs

1 tablespoon sugar

½ teaspoon salt

Clean giblets carefully, place in a saucepan, cover with cold water, and season with salt and pepper. Bring gradually to a boil, skim foam, cover pan, and simmer over low heat for 30 minutes.

Melt butter for the dumplings in a saucepan and add flour. Stir well, then add water and cook over high heat, stirring until the mixture is easily detachable from the sides of the pan and from the spoon. Remove pan from heat and knead the mixture for 10 minutes. Add 1 egg and knead well for another 10 minutes. Mix in the other egg. Stir in sugar and salt. Drop teaspoons of the mixture, 1 at a time, into boiling water and cook until dumplings rise to the surface. Drain in a colander and pour cold water over.

Add apples, prunes, carrots and celery, and leeks or onion to the soup pot and simmer until fruits and vegetables are very tender, about 30 minutes. Add sugar and vinegar, and serve with flour dumplings. *Serves 4.*

Lauritz Melchior (1890–1973), regarded as the greatest Wagnerian tenor of this century, sang at the Met for twenty-four seasons. This family recipe is by Kirstin Jensen, who raised Melchior and his siblings. She later published a cookbook which helped pay for Melchior's musical education.

ABOVE: *A party with (left to right) Giovanni Martinelli, Elisabeth Rethberg, Lauritz Melchior, Mrs. Melchior, Kirsten Flagstad, Dorothee Manski (with dog), and Emanuel List.* OPPOSITE: *Mr. and Mrs. Melchior celebrate their silver wedding anniversary.*

Bruce Crawford
Leek and Watercress Soup

3 medium leeks (white part only)
1 small onion
2 tablespoons (¼ stick) butter
3 medium potatoes, peeled and thinly sliced
3 cups chicken broth
1 bunch watercress
1 cup milk
1 cup heavy cream
Salt and pepper to taste

Cut leeks in half lengthwise, then rinse well to remove any dirt or sand. Thinly slice leeks and onion. In a saucepan, heat butter and sauté leeks and onion until light golden. Add potatoes and broth, and bring to a boil. Reduce heat, cover, and simmer for 30 minutes. Remove watercress leaves from stems. After the soup has simmered for 15 minutes, add the watercress leaves (reserve a few for garnish) and simmer for the remaining 15 minutes.

Puree the soup mixture in a blender until perfectly smooth. Return to pan, add milk to thin, and stir and simmer for 5 more minutes; do not let boil. Add cream, then season with salt and pepper. Garnish with a few watercress leaves and serve hot or chilled. *Serves 6.*

Salvatore Baccaloni feeds the poor in La Forza del Destino.

Bruce Crawford is the General Manager of the Metropolitan Opera. He and his wife Chris live in Manhattan. She notes: "This soup is almost a meal in itself. It is good as a supper served with a mixed salad of endive, bibb lettuce, arugula, shredded carrots, radishes, and tomatoes, with an oil and vinegar and garlic dressing, warmed French bread, and fruit for dessert. Or it is good as a first course. We find it better than the best ice cream and always look upon it as a treat down to the last drop. And it's best cold."

Frederica von Stade
Soupe à Sara

1 medium onion, grated
1 tablespoon butter
1 (10-ounce) package frozen green peas
1 (10¾-ounce) can beef consommé mixed with 1
  can water
1 tablespoon sugar
1 teaspoon (scant) dried leaf thyme
Pinch of garlic powder
1 cup heavy cream
½ cup milk
Croutons
½ cup Champagne (optional)

In a saucepan, cook onion in butter until soft and transparent, about 5 minutes. Stir often, being careful not to burn it. Add the peas and con- sommé, bring to a simmer, and cook over low heat for 10 minutes.

Add sugar, thyme, and garlic powder; stir and cook for another few minutes. Put the mixture in an electric blender, add the cream and milk, and blend to desired consistency. Serve chilled or hot with croutons. For those who have a bottle in the fridge, add an optional ½ cup Cham- pagne. *Serves 4.*

Frederica von Stade
has sung leading mezzo-soprano
roles with the Met since her debut in
1970. She is a favorite in opera
houses around the world, and has
been seen in "Live From the Met"
telecasts of Hansel and Gretel, Le
Nozze di Figaro, *and* Idomeneo.

Bonisolli's Super Spaghetti Seafood Special
Franco Bonisolli

Pennoni al Tonno
Luciano Pavarotti

Pasta with White Clam Sauce
alla Della Vecchia
Johanna Meier

Tagliatelle with Walnut Sauce
Renata Scotto

Pasta with Peas
Linda J. Freitag

Penne ai Broccoli
Leo Nucci

Pasta with Pesto alla Boccanegra
John W. Freeman

Pasta with Healthy Tomato Sauce
Italo Tajo

Spaghetti Chaliapin
Mrs. Schuyler G. Chapin

Risotto al Barolo
Ugo Benelli

Risotto alla Paesana
con Cavolo e Fagioli Rossi
Franco Corelli

Green Lasagna alla Bolognese
Brenda Boozer

Swiss Chard and Ricotta Ravioli
with Porcini Sauce
Wally and Charles Riecker

OPPOSITE: *Rosa Ponselle.* OVERLEAF: *Renata Scotto's Tagliatelle with Walnut Sauce, and the comb and fan she used in* Madama Butterfly. *Miss Scotto is shown as Cio-Cio-San.*

PASTA AND RICE DISHES

Franco Bonisolli

Bonisolli's Super Spaghetti Seafood Special

12 littleneck clams (or more, if desired)

8 large mussels

4 cloves garlic, 3 cut in slivers and 1 minced

2 tablespoons chopped fresh parsley

2 tablespoons olive oil

6 cherry tomatoes

Pinch of red pepper flakes, or to taste

4 small squid, cleaned and cut into rings

*4 jumbo shrimp, shelled and cut into large pieces;
    plus 4 jumbo shrimp, left whole*

1 pound spaghetti or vermicelli

Minced fresh parsley

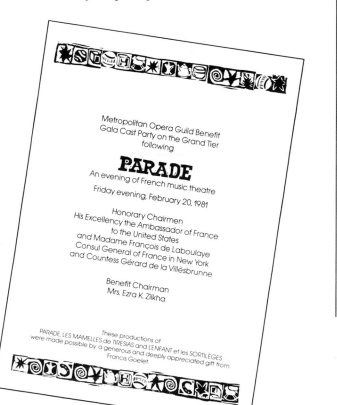

Metropolitan Opera Guild Benefit
Gala Cast Party on the Grand Tier
following

PARADE

An evening of French music theatre

Friday evening, February 20, 1981

Honorary Chairmen
His Excellency the Ambassador of France
to the United States
and Madame François de Laboulaye
Consul General of France in New York
and Countess Gérard de la Villèsbrunne

Benefit Chairman
Mrs. Ezra K. Zilkha

These productions of
PARADE, LES MAMELLES de TIRESIAS and L'ENFANT et les SORTILÈGES
were made possible by a generous and deeply appreciated gift from
Francis Goelet

Brush clams and mussels under cold water to remove sand and beards. Place in a saucepan, add 3 slivered garlic, parsley, and 1 tablespoon oil. Cover and cook over high heat until shells open, about 10 minutes. Remove seafood from shells and reserve. Strain broth into a bowl.

In a skillet, place remaining tablespoon oil, the remaining garlic, tomatoes, and red pepper flakes; add the strained broth of the shellfish, cover, and cook over low heat for a few minutes. Add squid and shrimp and cook until shrimp turn pink, about 3 minutes; do not overcook. Add cooked clams and mussels and heat through. Remove and reserve the 4 whole shrimp.

In the meantime, cook pasta in boiling water, using very little or no salt, since the seafood and their juices are quite salty. Cook until just *al dente*, drain well, and add to skillet. Mix rapidly using 2 large wooden forks over high heat so that the juices can be quickly absorbed, without getting too dry. Make sure the pasta stays *al dente*. Serve immediately on warmed plates, garnished with whole shrimp, mussel shells, and parsley. *Serves 4.*

Franco Bonisolli
has sung leading tenor roles at the
Met since his debut in 1971. "This
dish can be a complete meal. I
purposely added very little fat, since
it really does not need it, and that
way the calories are limited (if you
like, you can add more olive oil).
But whoever dares add Parmesan or
meatballs shall be sent to the firing
squad with Cavaradossi!"

Luciano Pavarotti
Pennoni al Tonno

2 tablespoons corn oil

⅓ cup finely chopped onion

3 (6½-ounce) cans imported tuna (Italian or
   Spanish), packed in oil

1 (2-ounce) can anchovies, cut small

½ (6-ounce) can tomato paste

1 (12-ounce) can tomato juice

Garlic salt to taste

1½ cups grated Parmesan cheese

1 pound pennoni or other pasta, cooked until al
   dente

In a saucepan, heat oil and sauté onion until transparent. Add the tuna and anchovies, and stir for 2 or 3 minutes. Add the tomato paste, tomato juice, and garlic salt. Stir well and simmer for 15 minutes. Add sauce to cooked pasta, mix well, and sprinkle on grated cheese. Serve immediately. *Serves 6.*

Luciano Pavarotti
still lives part of the time in the town
of his birth, Modena, Italy, when he
is not singing all over the world.
One of the best-known singers opera
has ever produced, he first sang at
the Met in 1968, and has since
performed 16 roles more than 160
times for the company. He has
written "One of the very nicest
things about life is the way we must
regularly stop whatever it is we are
doing and devote our attention to
eating," and is known to be quite a
chef himself.

*Luciano
Pavarotti.*

Johanna Meier
Pasta with White Clam Sauce alla Della Vecchia

½ cup (1 stick) butter
½ cup olive oil
4 cloves garlic, crushed
Pinch of saffron threads, crushed
¼ teaspoon dried thyme
¼ cup chopped fresh parsley
Pinch of dried oregano
2 teaspoons crushed mustard seed (in a mortar or processor)
1 small hot chili pepper, or less to taste
2 (6½-ounce) cans baby clams, drained
6 fresh littleneck clams, well scrubbed
1 pound pasta

In a heavy pan, place butter and oil over medium heat. When hot, add garlic and sauté for a minute or two; *don't let the garlic brown.* Add all remaining ingredients except clams and pasta, and cook gently for about 10 minutes. Add the clams to the sauce, and cook until the shells have opened, about 5 minutes. Cook pasta until *al dente,* then pour clam sauce over. *Serves 4.*

Johanna Meier
has sung many roles at the Met since her company debut in 1976, including Ariadne, Senta, Isolde, Fidelio, and Elisabeth. This recipe is a favorite of hers, submitted by her husband, Guido Della Vecchia. They live in South Dakota.

Renata Scotto
Tagliatelle with Walnut Sauce

¼ cup olive oil
1 cup coarsely crushed walnuts
½ cup good (homemade) tomato sauce
½ cup clarified butter
Salt and pepper to taste
1 cup strong chicken broth
1 pound tagliatelle, cooked until al dente
1 cup freshly grated Parmesan cheese

In a saucepan, heat oil over low heat, add walnuts, and sauté for 2 or 3 minutes. Add tomato sauce, clarified butter, salt, and pepper. Mix well, and bring to a slow simmer. Immediately add chicken broth and cook over very low heat until the sauce gets a good consistency, about 15 minutes.

To serve, first mix cooked tagliatelle with a generous amount of cheese, then mix with walnut sauce and serve remaining grated cheese on the side. *Serves 6.*

Renata Scotto
is from Savona, Italy, and has sung at the Met since 1965, performing

Renata Scotto.

over 230 times in twenty-five roles.
Her "Live From the Met" television
appearances include the first program, La Bohème, *as well as*
Otello, Luisa Miller, Don Carlo,
Manon Lescaut, *and* Francesca da
Rimini. *She says, "To me, cooking
is an artistic experience, bringing
into focus all the senses, the balance
of proportion, the discipline of tech-
nique and, very importantly, a dash*

*of daring—you see, even in the
cucina I cannot resist a touch of
bravura.*

*"I don't profess to be a great chef,
but there is little else in life that I
find more relaxing or enjoyable than
preparing a wonderful dinner for my
family, or sharing an evening at
home with my friends over a meal,
the principal ingredient of which is
love."*

Linda J. Freitag
Pasta with Peas
(THE "P" DISH)

1 pound pasta (small shapes)
¼ cup olive oil
1 medium onion, chopped
3 cloves garlic, minced
1 red bell pepper, seeded and diced
⅓ cup dry vermouth
½ teaspoon dried oregano
Salt and pepper to taste
1 (10-ounce) package frozen peas
⅓ cup pignoli (pine nuts)
3 tablespoons chopped fresh parsley
⅓ cup grated Parmesan cheese, approximately

Cook pasta in lightly salted water until just done (al dente). Drain well.

In the meantime, heat oil in a skillet, and sauté onion and garlic until transparent and soft, about 5 minutes; do not brown. Add diced pepper and sauté for another 2 or 3 minutes. Add vermouth, then season with oregano and salt and pepper to taste. Raise heat to medium, add peas, stir until defrosted, and cook until peas are done, about 3 or 4 minutes. Stir in pignoli and parsley, cook for another minute, then toss well with hot pasta. Sprinkle with cheese when serving. *Serves 4.*

Linda J. Freitag
is the Employment Coordinator for
the Personnel Department of the
Metropolitan Opera.

Leo Nucci
Penne ai Broccoli

¼ cup olive oil
1 tablespoon crushed hot red pepper flakes
1 clove garlic, minced
Salt
1½ cups bite-size broccoli florets
1 tablespoon butter
8 ounces penne (tube pasta)
1 teaspoon finely minced fresh parsley
Freshly grated Parmesan or Romano Cheese (optional)

In a skillet, heat oil, add red pepper flakes, garlic, a pinch of salt, and the broccoli. Stir and sauté, adding the butter after 2 or 3 minutes. The broccoli should be crisp, not overcooked. Keep warm. Cook the pasta until al dente, drain well, then add to broccoli and mix well. Serve hot, sprinkled with parsley and cheese, if desired. *Serves 4.*

Leo Nucci
sang at La Scala, Vienna, and
Covent Garden before making his
Met debut in 1980. Since then he
has returned many times. He lives in Lodi, Italy.

John W. Freeman
Pasta with Pesto alla Boccanegra

5 cups fresh basil, large stems removed
1 cup olive oil, preferably extra-virgin
½ cup fresh parsley, large stems removed
1–2 large cloves garlic
3 tablespoons pignoli (pine nuts) or pistachios
3 tablespoons grated Parmesan cheese, plus additional for serving
1 tablespoon sesame salt, or 2 teaspoons coarse (kosher) salt
1 teaspoon ground black (Java or Italian style) pepper
1½ pounds pasta (capellini, rotelle, tortellini)

Wash, then drain and trim basil. Place olive oil in the bowl of an electric blender. Add enough parsley, basil, and garlic to fill blender to top, loosely packed. Switch on the medium (chop) setting, and push down leaves with a rubber spatula if needed. When basil is partially chopped, add remaining basil (if any), then nuts, using spatula as before, and finally the cheese, sesame salt, and pepper. Blend only long enough to produce a coarse, grainy mixture, with small particles still visible.

Do not heat pesto sauce, as this would destroy flavor. Keep refrigerated, bringing to room temperature before use.

When ready to serve, cook pasta until *al dente*. Serve in shallow soup plates with additional cheese if desired. *Serves 6.*

Note Chopped tomatoes are also a recommended addition to this dish. Leftover pesto sauce will keep in the refrigerator for about a week if tightly covered and topped with a thin layer of olive oil. If frozen, it can be kept up to a year.

John W. Freeman is an Associate Editor of Opera News, *and is the author of* The Metropolitan Opera—Stories of the Great Operas.

Salvatore Baccaloni.

Italo Tajo
Pasta with Healthy Tomato Sauce

2 pounds fresh (Italian) pear tomatoes or canned,
    drained plum tomatoes
2 medium carrots, peeled and cut into 2-inch
    pieces
2 medium onions, quartered
2 cloves garlic, crushed
2 celery stalks, trimmed and cut into 2-inch
    pieces
3 sprigs parsley
¼ cup fresh basil leaves, or 1 teaspoon dried
½ cup water
Pinch of hot red pepper flakes
1½ pounds pasta
Grated Parmesan cheese
Extra-virgin olive oil or melted butter

In a large saucepan, combine vegetables, herbs, water, and red pepper flakes. Bring to a boil, reduce heat, cover, and simmer for about 1½ hours. Puree the mixture in a food processor or blender, then return to the pan and cook over low heat until sauce thickens slightly, about 30 minutes. Stir a few times to prevent scorching.

To serve, cook pasta until *al dente*, then drain well. Pour sauce over pasta, add cheese to taste, and lightly coat with olive oil or melted butter. *Serves 6 to 8.*

Italo Tajo made his Met debut in 1948, left in 1950, returned in 1976, and has remained with the company ever since, singing such roles as Alcindoro and Benoit in La Bohème *and the Sacristan in* Tosca. *He lives in Cincinnati and New York City.*

Mrs. Schuyler G. Chapin
Spaghetti Chaliapin

1 ounce dried porcini (cèpes) mushrooms
½ pound (2 sticks) butter
1 (6-ounce) can tomato paste
½ pound bacon, fried crisp, drained, and
    crumbled
½ cup beef broth
2 pounds spaghetti
Salt and pepper to taste
½ cup grated Parmesan cheese

Soak the mushrooms for 2 hours in hot water to cover. Drain, strain liquid, and reserve. Chop the softened mushrooms.

In a saucepan, melt butter, add tomato paste, and blend well over low heat. Add chopped mushrooms, crumbled bacon, beef broth, and ½ cup of the strained mushroom water. Cover and simmer for 10 minutes, then add a little more mushroom liquid if too thick.

Cook spaghetti until just done (*al dente*). Drain well, place in a bowl or serving dish, mix with the sauce, toss, and add salt and pepper and as much Parmesan as desired. *Serves 8.*

Note Should there be any left over, this spaghetti is even better the next day, reheated in a double boiler.

*Mrs. Schuyler G. Chapin
is a member of the Metropolitan
Opera Guild's Board of Directors,
and her husband was the General
Manager of the Met for several
years. "This recipe was given to us
as a wedding present by Mrs. Sergei
Rachmaninoff. I don't really know
what the Chaliapin connection was,
but I like to think about the after-
concert parties where it was served."*

Ugo Benelli
Risotto al Barolo

4 cups Italian Arborio rice
1½ bottles Barolo (dry red wine)
10 tablespoons (1¼ sticks) butter
2 tablespoons olive oil
7 ounces smoked pancetta (Italian smoked bacon), chopped

7 ounces sweet Italian sausage, casings removed and meat crumbled
1 large onion, thinly sliced
Grated Parmesan cheese

In a large bowl, cover the rice with wine. Let soak for 2 to 3 hours.

In a large, wide pan, heat ½ cup (1 stick) butter and the oil. Add pancetta, crumbled sausage meat, and onion, and cook over low heat until onion is very soft, about 10 minutes; stir often. Add the soaked rice and the remaining wine, bring to a simmer, and cook over low heat, stirring constantly, for 8 to 10 minutes, adding more wine if mixture is too dry.

When rice is cooked, blend in remaining butter. Top with a generous amount of grated cheese. *Serves 6 to 8.*

Note Mr. Benelli uses a heatproof terracotta pan to make this risotto.

*Ugo Benelli
was born in Genoa. He made his
Met debut in 1986 as Don Basilio in
Le Nozze di Figaro.*

Franco Corelli

Risotto alla Paesana con Cavolo e Fagioli Rossi

PEASANT-STYLE RISOTTO

1 head green cabbage
2 tablespoons olive oil
3 tablespoons butter
1 medium onion, chopped
2 sweet Italian sausages, casings removed
2 slices pancetta (Italian unsmoked bacon),
    chopped
3 cloves garlic, 1 chopped
1 tablespoon minced fresh parsley
2 tomatoes, peeled, seeded, and chopped
1½ cups Italian Arborio rice
2 cups beef or chicken broth, heated to boiling
Salt and pepper to taste
1 (10-ounce) can red kidney beans, drained
2 tablespoons grated Parmesan cheese

Trim cabbage, cut in half, and remove core. Place in boiling water and cook until almost tender, about 7 minutes. Drain well, chop, and reserve.

In a deep saucepan, heat oil and half the butter. Add onion, sausage meat, pancetta, whole and chopped garlic, and parsley. Mix well and sauté for a few minutes. When the whole garlic cloves turn golden, remove and discard them. Add the tomatoes and continue cooking for 2 or 3 minutes, stirring a few times.

Add the rice, boiling broth, and chopped cabbage. Season with salt and pepper. Bring to a boil, reduce heat, cover, and cook gently for about 12 minutes. Add the kidney beans, remaining butter, and Parmesan. Stir and mix with a fork, cover again, and cook gently for a few minutes until rice and cabbage are done. Serve with additional grated cheese on the side. *Serves 6.*

Franco Corelli
first sang with the Met in 1961, and
appeared there every year until
1974, thrilling audiences in such
roles as Calaf, Manrico, Werther,
and Rodolfo. He lives in New York.

Franco Corelli.

Brenda Boozer
Green Lasagna alla Bolognese

Meat Sauce

5 slices lean bacon, chopped
3 medium onions, chopped
2 carrots, peeled and chopped
2 celery stalks, chopped with leaves
2 pounds boneless beef round, chopped
2 cups dry red wine, approximately
2 cups beef broth or water
1 (32-ounce) can Italian plum tomatoes
1 large clove garlic, minced
2 tablespoons chopped fresh parsley
2 tablespoons chopped fresh basil, or 1½
    teaspoons dried
Salt to taste
Freshly ground black pepper to taste
½ teaspoon grated nutmeg
2 tablespoons tomato paste

Béchamel Sauce

½ cup (1 stick) butter
½ cup flour
4–5 cups hot milk
¼ teaspoon grated nutmeg
Salt and pepper to taste

Lasagna

¼ cup (½ stick) butter
2 tablespoons salt
1½ pounds green lasagna noodles
½ pound Parmesan cheese, grated

Prepare meat sauce first. In a heavy saucepan, sauté chopped bacon for a minute or two to render fat. Add onions, carrots, and celery and sauté for 10 minutes, stirring often. Add meat, mix, and break up lumps with a fork. Sauté until meat is browned, stirring often, about 5 minutes. Add 1 cup red wine, the beef broth, and all remaining ingredients. Cover and simmer for 1 hour. Add more red wine if mixture gets too dry.

While meat sauce simmers, prepare béchamel. In a heavy saucepan, heat butter, stir in flour, and cook while stirring until smooth and foaming; do not let brown. Slowly add 4 cups milk, while stirring. Stir until smooth and thickened, then season with nutmeg and salt and pepper. If sauce gets too thick, add more hot milk.

Preheat oven to 350 degrees. In a large saucepan, bring about 2 gallons of water to a full boil. Add 1 tablespoon butter and the salt. Drop lasagna strips, one by one, into the boiling water. Stir with a wooden spoon to keep them from sticking, and boil for 8 to 10 minutes. Drain in a colander, and rinse quickly under cold water. Drain again, place lasagna separately on towels, and pat dry.

Butter a large (about 9 × 14–inch) baking dish, about 3 inches high. Cover the bottom with lasagna, then add a layer of the meat sauce. Spoon in ¼ cup of béchamel and sprinkle with grated cheese. Repeat alternating layers until pan is filled. Cover the last layer of lasagna with meat sauce, béchamel, and cheese, then dot with remaining butter. Bake until top is well browned and crusty, about 30 to 40 minutes. Remove from oven, let sit for 5 minutes, then serve. *Serves 8 to 10.*

Brenda Boozer
made her Met debut on Christmas
Day, 1979, as Hansel in Hansel
and Gretel, and since has sung
other important mezzo roles with
the company. She lives in a small
town in upstate New York with her
husband, the actor and comedian
Robert Klein.

Wally and Charles Riecker
Swiss Chard and Ricotta Ravioli with Porcini Sauce

Ravioli
4–5 cups flour
6 eggs
½ cup water
1 tablespoon olive oil
1 egg yolk, lightly beaten

Semolina
3 tablespoons salt
Grated Parmesan cheese, for serving

Filling
1 bunch Swiss chard
1½ pounds ricotta cheese
½ cup grated Parmesan cheese
Salt and white pepper to taste

Sauce
2 cups beef broth
2 cups chicken broth
½ cup dry white wine
2 ounces dried porcini (cèpes) mushrooms,
*   chopped*
1 cup (2 sticks) butter
1 cup chopped fresh parsley
½ cup chopped fresh basil, or 2 tablespoons dried
Salt and pepper to taste
1 cup grated Parmesan cheese
1 pint heavy cream

Prepare the dough for the ravioli. Sift the flour onto a board. Make a well in the center, add eggs and water, and work until the dough begins to form a large ball. Knead the dough for 5 to 8 minutes; add more flour while kneading if the dough feels too sticky. When dough is elastic to the touch and springs back when poked with your finger, put a tablespoon of olive oil in your hand and coat the ball of dough with it.

Place dough in a bowl, cover, and refrigerate for 4 to 5 hours.

While dough chills, prepare the filling. Remove the stems from the Swiss chard, chop the leaves, and blanch in boiling water for 2 minutes. Drain well, removing as much water as possible. In a bowl, combine the ricotta with the chopped chard, add Parmesan cheese, and season with salt and pepper. Mix until well blended. Keep chilled until ready to use.

Remove ravioli dough from refrigerator 1 hour before shaping. For the sauce, bring the broths and wine to a boil in a saucepan, transfer the mixture to a bowl, add the chopped porcini, and let soak for 1 hour.

When dough is room temperature, roll out in even strips, using the thinnest setting of a pasta machine. (I admit that I have never used a rolling pin to roll out the dough; if you do, roll it out quite thin, in long strips 2 to 3 inches wide.) With a pastry brush, paint the edges of the strips with the beaten egg yolk. Place heaping teaspoons of filling on the strip, about 1½ inches apart, then cover the strip with another strip of dough the same size. Press down the edges of the strip to seal well, then press down between and

around the mounds of filling to eliminate air pockets. With a ravioli cutter, cut the filled strips into individual squares. Set the ravioli on a baking sheet sprinkled with semolina to avoid sticking while you prepare remaining squares.

To cook ravioli, bring about 6 quarts of water to a boil, add salt, and cook the ravioli, not too many at a time (about 30 to 35) for 8 to 10 minutes. Drain well in a colander.

While ravioli are cooking, prepare sauce. In a 2-quart saucepan, melt butter, add the broths and porcini, and heat but do not let boil. Add herbs, salt and pepper, then, while constantly stirring, the cheese and the cream. When you add the cream, turn off the heat. Stir until well blended. Place drained ravioli in a serving bowl and pour the sauce over. Mix and serve, with more cheese on the side. *Serves 6 to 8.*

Wally Riecker has worked for the Special Events Department of the Met, and served as the recipe coordinator for this book. She is the daughter of the late Met conductor Fausto Cleva. Her husband, Charles Riecker, is the Coordinator for Artists Relations at the Met.

Quick and Easy Fish Filets
Brigitte Fassbaender

Fish Medallions
Jean Kraft

Brook Trout in Red Wine
Bernd Weikl

Filet of Flounder with Peas
Franco Corelli

Clams alla Marinara
Luciano Pavarotti

Matelotte d'Anguille Caruso

Crabmeat Casserole
Max Rudolf

Zarzuela de Mariscos
Plácido Domingo

Scallops au Gratin
Jeffrey Hildt

Shrimp Gumbo
Leontyne Price

Dad's Lobster Newburg à la *Pandora I*
Mrs. Gilbert W. Humphrey

Shrimp Creole
Elinor Harper

Shrimp Casserole
Mrs. Peter F. Packard

OVERLEAF: *Plácido Domingo's Zarzuela de Mariscos, and the sword he used in* Otello. *Mr. Domingo is shown as Otello.*

SEAFOOD

SOUVENIR
MENU

METROPOLITAN
OPERA ASSOCIATION, Inc.

EDWARD JOHNSON
General Manager

EDWARD ZIEGLER
Ass't. General Manager

EARLE R. LEWIS
Ass't. General Manager

SPECIAL TRAIN

En Route

DALLAS TO ATLANTA

APRIL 27, 1941

Brigitte Fassbaender
Quick and Easy Fish Filets

1 cup Champagne (or sparkling white wine, but
    Champagne does make a difference)
2 teaspoons Madras curry powder
Juice of 1 lemon
Salt and pepper to taste
4 firm fish filets (monkfish, tilefish, or other),
    about 2 pounds
2 tablespoons (¼ stick) butter
3 medium onions, minced
Finely chopped fresh dill

Combine the Champagne, curry powder, lemon juice, and salt and pepper. Marinate fish in this mixture for 45 minutes.

In a large skillet or shallow pan, heat butter and sauté onions until soft and transparent about 5 minutes; do not let brown. Add fish and marinade and simmer until fish is just cooked, about 10 to 15 minutes. Add more Champagne during cooking if needed.

Garnish with dill and serve on a bed of wild rice or (for the diet-conscious) with green beans or broccoli. *Serves 4.*

*Brigitte Fassbaender
sings leading mezzo roles at Covent
Garden, Salzburg, Paris, Milan,
and Vienna, as well as at the Met.
She lives in Munich. "I don't eat*
*any red meat, but love fish of all
kinds. I also love to cook, but never
have time for lengthy preparations;
so my 'creations' are always rather
improvised, like this simple fish
dish."*

Jean Kraft
Fish Medallions

1 pound scrod or haddock filets
1 cup heavy cream
1½ cups fresh white bread crumbs (without crust)
Salt and pepper to taste
¼ teaspoon grated nutmeg
¼ cup (½ stick) butter

Cut the fish into chunks, put in the bowl of a food processor, and process while adding cream, bread crumbs, salt and pepper, and nutmeg. When well processed, shape into large patties. In a skillet, heat butter and sauté medallions until nicely browned on both sides, about 10 minutes. (If using a nonstick skillet, decrease the amount of butter.) *Serves 2 to 4.*

*Jean Kraft
has sung mezzo roles at the Met
since 1970. "This is a very fast,
very light meal. I often just steam
broccoli and even have a side of
potato salad to complete the meal."*

Bernd Weikl
Brook Trout in Red Wine

4 large trout, cleaned and dressed
Juice of 1 lemon
Salt and pepper to taste
¼ cup flour
¼ cup (½ stick) butter
⅓ cup slivered almonds
½ cup dry red wine
1 scant teaspoon cornstarch
1 tablespoon water
2 tablespoons minced fresh parsley

Preheat broiler. Dip trout in lemon juice, sprinkle with salt and pepper, and dredge in flour. In a heavy skillet, heat 3 tablespoons of the butter and sauté fish until nicely browned on both sides, about 5 minutes. Meanwhile, brown almonds in another pan in remaining butter. Set aside.

When fish are done, arrange on a heat-proof serving platter and keep warm. Deglaze skillet with red wine and cook down to about ⅓ cup. Dissolve cornstarch in 1 tablespoon water, add to skillet, and stir to thicken. Correct seasoning, pour over fish, scatter almonds over all, and glaze under broiler for 1 minute. Sprinkle with minced parsley. *Serves 4.*

Bernd Weikl
began his career in Hanover, and sang at Hamburg and Bayreuth before coming to the Met in 1977. Since then he has sung baritone roles in Wagner and Strauss operas, as well as in Beethoven's Fidelio.

Franco Corelli
Filet of Flounder with Peas

1½ tablespoons olive oil
2 tablespoons (¼ stick) butter
1 tablespoon chopped fresh basil
3 scallions (green and white parts), chopped
1 clove garlic, minced, plus 4 whole garlic cloves
1 teaspoon drained capers
1 (10-ounce) package frozen peas
4 large flounder filets, about ½ pound each

In a deep skillet, heat oil and butter, then add the chopped ingredients, whole garlic, and capers. Sauté while stirring over low heat. When garlic cloves turn golden, remove and discard. Add peas to skillet, simmer for 5 minutes, then add the filets. Cook for 2 minutes, turn very carefully, and cook for another 2 minutes or so—don't overcook. Remove fish to a hot serving dish. If pan juices are too thin, reduce very quickly over high heat. Season to taste, then spoon over fish and serve. *Serves 4.*

Luciano Pavarotti
Clams alla Marinara

1½ dozen littleneck clams
⅓ cup water
¼ cup olive oil
1 small onion, chopped
2 cloves garlic, minced
¾ cup dry white wine
Juice of ½ lemon
Cayenne pepper to taste
Salt to taste
Coarsely ground black pepper to taste
3 tablespoons chopped fresh parsley

Rinse the clams under cold water and scrub the shells with a stiff brush. Place clams in a saucepan, add water, and bring to a boil. Cover the pan and steam clams open. Remove the clams just as they open and reserve in a bowl. Strain the clam juice through a triple-layer cheesecloth and reserve.

In a deep saucepan, heat oil, add onion and garlic, and sauté until they start to color, about 5 minutes. Add the wine, strained clam juice, and lemon juice, and season with cayenne, salt, and pepper. Bring to a boil, simmer for 10 minutes, then add the clams and simmer for 2 more minutes. Serve sprinkled with parsley. *Serves 1 to 2.*

OPPOSITE: *Enrico Caruso.*

Matelotte d'Anguille Caruso

1 eel, 1½–2 pounds
1 large onion
1 clove garlic
2 tablespoons (¼ stick) butter
1 teaspoon flour
¾ cup dry red wine
1 cup fresh button mushrooms
1 pint oyster liquid
Cayenne pepper
Salt
1 bay leaf
1 sprig thyme
Croutons

Clean and skin the eel, then cut into 1-inch pieces. Chop onion and garlic until fine, and sauté in butter. When onion begins to brown, add flour. Gradually pour in the wine and add the mushrooms. Stir in oyster liquid and cook slowly for 10 minutes. Season to taste with cayenne and salt, then add the bay leaf and thyme. Bring liquid to a boil, then add the eel. Lower heat, cover, and simmer for about 1 hour. Garnish with croutons and serve. *Serves 6.*

This is a favorite Enrico Caruso recipe from Antoine's restaurant in New Orleans.

Max Rudolf
Crabmeat Casserole

½ cup (1 stick) butter
2 tablespoons flour
2 cups hot milk
1 teaspoon lemon juice
1 teaspoon Worcestershire sauce
1 teaspoon dry mustard
Tabasco to taste
Salt to taste
1 pound lump crabmeat
2 celery stalks (white part only), minced
1 tablespoon grated onion
¾ cup fine dry bread crumbs
Sprigs of parsley
Lemon wedges

Preheat oven to 375 degrees. Place butter in the top of a double boiler and put over simmering water. Stir in flour until smooth. Gradually add hot milk, stirring until smooth and thickened, then blend in lemon juice, Worcestershire sauce, mustard, and Tabasco and salt. Combine the sauce with remaining ingredients, reserving ¼ cup of the bread crumbs. Put the mixture in a lightly buttered medium casserole or into individual shells, sprinkle top with reserved bread crumbs, and bake until lightly browned, about 20 minutes. Garnish and serve. *Serves 4.*

Max Rudolf was a conductor at the Met for fifteen seasons, beginning in 1945, leading 130 performances. He and his wife, Liese, whose recipe this is, live in Philadelphia. "This is one of our favorite dishes. We especially enjoy it during our summers in Maine."

Plácido Domingo
Zarzuela de Mariscos

3 tablespoons olive oil
3 tablespoons butter
1 cup finely chopped onion
½ cup finely chopped green or red bell pepper
2 cloves garlic, minced
½ bay leaf
¼ teaspoon ground saffron, or ½ teaspoon threads
2 tablespoons lemon juice
½ cup dry white wine
1 pound ripe tomatoes, peeled, seeded, and chopped
2 cups water
1 pound rock lobster tails in the shell, each cut into 3 pieces
1 pound halibut filet, cut into chunks
½ pound mussels, well scrubbed and debearded
8 cherrystone clams
2 tablespoons minced fresh parsley, plus additional for garnish
1 teaspoon salt
Freshly ground black pepper to taste

¼ cup warmed brandy
Slices of Italian or French bread
Butter
Olive oil

In a heavy, 6-quart saucepan or Dutch oven, heat oil and butter. Add onion, pepper, and garlic and sauté over medium heat for about 5 minutes, stirring constantly; do not let brown. Add bay leaf, saffron, lemon juice, wine, tomatoes, and water. Mix well and bring to a boil. Add seafood, cover, and simmer until mussels and clams have opened and the lobster and halibut are cooked, about 5 to 7 minutes. Add parsley and season with salt and pepper. Ignite the warmed brandy and pour it over the mixture. Make croutons by browning ½-inch slices of Italian or French bread in butter and olive oil. Sprinkle with parsley. Ladle Zarzuela into broad soup plates and serve with croutons. *Serves 4.*

Plácido Domingo
is one of the world's leading tenors.
He was born in Madrid and raised
in Mexico. "This is a typical Span-
ish dish. It is named after the
zarzuela, a popular Spanish enter-
tainment that mixes musical num-
bers with spoken dialogue—a kind

of Spanish operetta. Like the
zarzuela, this dish has a little bit of
everything."

Jeffrey Hildt
Scallops au Gratin

1 pound sea scallops, cut in half
1 cup soda crackers or saltines, crumbled
1 cup grated cheddar cheese
1 cup fresh bread cubes
Salt and pepper to taste
½ pound fresh mushrooms, sliced
5 tablespoons butter
2 cups light cream or half-and-half

Preheat oven to 350 degrees. Rinse scallops, drain, and pat dry. Combine cracker crumbs, cheese, and bread cubes; season with salt and pepper. In a skillet, lightly sauté mushrooms in 2 tablespoons butter, then season with a few grindings of pepper.

Butter a 2-quart casserole. Add alternate layers of crumb mixture, sautéed mushrooms, and scallops. Pour in cream, and finish with a layer of cracker crumbs. Dot with remaining butter. Bake until top is well browned and bubbly, about 50 minutes. *Serves 4.*

Jeffrey Hildt
is the Associate Publisher of Opera
News *magazine.*

Leontyne Price
Shrimp Gumbo

5 tablespoons butter
½ cup chopped onion
3 tablespoons flour
4½ cups chicken broth
2½ cups canned tomatoes
Salt to taste

2 teaspoons minced fresh parsley
¼ teaspoon dried thyme
1 clove garlic, minced
2 bay leaves
2 cups cooked okra, fresh or frozen
1 teaspoon filé powder
18 large shrimp, peeled and deveined
1 (8-ounce) container frozen crabmeat, thawed
Cooked white rice

Heat 2 tablespoons butter in a saucepan, then sauté onion for 5 minutes; do not let brown or scorch. Add remaining butter and, when it is melted, blend in the flour. Gradually add the broth, stirring until smooth and thickened. Add tomatoes, salt, parsley, thyme, garlic, and bay leaves. Cover and simmer for 1 hour. Add okra, *filé*, shrimp, and crabmeat. Mix well and simmer for another 8 to 10 minutes. Serve over hot rice. *Serves 4 to 5.*

Leontyne Price
writes of this recipe, "My father's
eyes always had an extra glow when
my mother brought this delicious
dish to the table on Sunday after
church. I hope you will enjoy it as
well. Bon appétit!"

Mrs. Gilbert W. Humphrey
Dad's Lobster Newburg
à la Pandora I

½ cup (1 stick) butter
4 lobsters, about 1½ pounds each, boiled and
    shelled, meat chopped (or about 1½ pounds
    lump crabmeat)
1 cup heavy cream, approximately
2 teaspoons paprika, or more to taste

OPPOSITE: *Leontyne Price in her kitchen.*

Salt and pepper to taste
⅓ cup sherry (your best), or more
3 egg yolks, lightly beaten

In a heavy skillet (I use iron) melt butter over low heat. Add the lobster meat as soon as the butter has melted and stir gently until the lobster is warm. Add just enough cream to make a thick sauce, and heat while stirring. Season with paprika (quite a bit), salt, and pepper. When mixture is hot, slowly add sherry to taste (I use a lot). Just before serving, add beaten yolks and stir carefully over very gentle heat to prevent curdling. Serve immediately on hot toast. *Serves about 6.*

Note If you use cheap sherry, add a splash of brandy at the last minute.

Mrs. Gilbert W. Humphrey
is President of the Metropolitan
Opera Association, and a member of
the Board of Directors of the Metro-
politan Opera Guild. "I learned to
do this dish at the age of nine on our
sailboat Pandora I, and I still do it
the same way. It is foolproof, very
easy, and very rich and delicious
after a day under sail."

Régine Crespin at the fish market. OVERLEAF: *Franz Mazura, Kiri Te Kanawa, and David Rendall in* Die Fledermaus.

Elinor Harper
Shrimp Creole

2 pounds large shrimp
2 tablespoons (¼ stick) butter
2 medium onions, chopped
3 cloves garlic, crushed
2 (14-ounce) cans tomatoes, cut up and juice
  retained
Chopped fresh dill
Fresh or dried oregano
Garlic powder
Salt
Freshly ground black pepper
½ cup dry white wine
1 green pepper, seeded and diced
½ cup sour cream
Cooked white or brown rice

Shell and devein shrimp. In a saucepan, heat butter, add onions and garlic, and sauté while stirring until soft, about 5 minutes. Add tomatoes with their juice, mix well, and add an ample amount of herbs and seasonings. Simmer for 15 minutes, then add wine and green pepper and simmer for another few minutes. Add shrimp, cook quickly for about 1½ minutes, then add sour cream. Mix and heat through. Serve immediately over rice. *Serves 6.*

Elinor Harper
is a soprano in the Met Chorus,
where she has sung for more than
twenty-five years.

Mrs. Peter F. Packard
Shrimp Casserole

½ cup (1 stick) butter, plus additional for top of
  casserole
Fine dry plain bread crumbs
1 cup cooked white rice
½ pound cooked and shelled shrimp
4 medium ripe tomatoes, peeled and quartered
1 medium onion, minced
1 teaspoon Worcestershire sauce
Salt and pepper to taste

Preheat oven to 375 degrees. Melt butter. Coat the inside of a medium casserole with melted butter and sprinkle with bread crumbs. Combine remaining butter with all other ingredients, then pour mixture into the casserole. Sprinkle top with additional bread crumbs and dot with a few pats of butter. Bake until nicely browned, about 20 minutes. *Serves 4.*

Mrs. Peter F. Packard
is a member of the Board of Directors
of the Metropolitan Opera Guild,
and a Member of the Metropolitan
Opera Association. Her mother is
the singer Jarmila Novotná.

Beef Roast à la "Viva Voce"
Morley Meredith

Berliner Rouladen
Edda Moser

Veal Silviano
John Keenan

Viennese Beef Goulash
Otto Schenk

Crepes de Boeuf
Lily Pons

Gala Cold Veal Roast
Regina Resnik

Ossobuco alla Moffo
Anna Moffo

Beef Patties in Cream Sauce
P. Michael Nordberg

Vitello Tonnato
Robert Merrill

Lampaanpotka
Martti Talvela

Veal Goulash
Risë Stevens

Cypriot Pork and Cauliflower alla Loulla
Andrea Velis

Veal, Tomato, and Orange Stew
Martina Arroyo

Oxtail Stew
Alton E. Peters

Savory Veal in Cream Sauce
Inge Borkh

Saltimbocca alla Romana
Paolo Montarsolo

Party Veal
Leonie Rysanek

Pork Hocks à la Belge
José van Dam

Spareribs and Brown Cabbage
Joyce Rasmussen Balint

Mandarin Ham Slices
Phyllis Curtin

Braised Lamb Shanks
Dorothy Kirsten

Boiled Tongue with Raisin Sauce
Zachary Solov

Boiled Beef Tongue with Polish Sauce
Helen Traubel

Marton Family's Layered Cabbage
Eva Marton

Djuveč
Zinka Milanov

Braised Meat Loaf
Fedora Barbieri

MEAT DISHES

Richard and Sara Tucker barbeque for their visitors, Christa Ludwig and Walter Berry. OVERLEAF: *Regina Resnik's Gala Cold Veal Roast, and the comb and fan she used in* Carmen. *Miss Resnik is shown as Donna Anna.*

Morley Meredith
Beef Roast
à la "Viva Voce"

3½-pound beef pot roast
Salt and pepper to taste
Ground ginger
¼ cup olive oil
3 large onions, thinly sliced
1 clove garlic, crushed
½ cup red Burgundy wine
12 pitted prunes, diced
2 cups hot weak tea
Cranberry gelatin (optional)
Oranges, cut in half and pulp removed
   (optional)
Watercress (optional)
1 (2-ounce) can mushrooms, drained and warmed
1 (4½-ounce) jar pitted green olives, drained

Preheat oven to 300 degrees. Sprinkle roast generously with salt, pepper, and ginger. In a skillet, heat oil over medium heat and sauté onions and garlic, stirring often, until light golden brown and soft, about 5 minutes. Place the seasoned roast in a Dutch oven or casserole and add the onion mixture and wine. Cover and bake for 2 hours.

Cover the prunes with hot tea and let stand until cold. Drain away all but ¼ cup of the liquid. After the meat has roasted for 2 hours, add the prunes, reserved prune liquid, and olives to the roast. Cover again and cook until the meat is tender, about 2 more hours.

Place roast on a serving platter. Surround the roast with a fresh cranberry gelatin served in halved orange shells and placed on a bed of watercress. Intersperse the mushrooms, prunes, and olives among the oranges. *Serves 6.*

*Morley Meredith
sang at the New York City Opera
before coming to the Met in 1962.
He has performed in every Met
season since then, singing over 400
performances of more than thirty-five
roles. Of this recipe, he adds "This
makes a delicious flavor combina-
tion, and it's so easy to prepare!"*

Edda Moser
Berliner Rouladen
BEEF ROLLS

8 slices boneless beef shoulder or round (about 4
   by 6 inches, ⅓ inch thick)
Salt to taste
Coarsely ground black pepper to taste
2 tablespoons Dijon mustard
8 thin slices lean smoked bacon
4 small onions, halved
8 small pickles or cornichons
3 tablespoons butter
4 cups hot water, or 2 cups water, 2 cups beef
   broth

Pat beef slices dry with paper towels, then pound them with a mallet or meat pounder. Season the slices with salt and pepper and spread one side lightly with mustard. Place a slice of bacon on each beef slice, then put half an onion and a pickle in the center. Roll up the slices, tuck in the ends, and tie securely or close with skewers.

Heat butter in a pan large enough to hold the rolls in 1 layer. Add the beef rolls, brown them lightly on one side, turn and brown the other side. Add enough hot water to come to the top of the rolls, cover the pan, and cook over low heat until meat is done, about 2 hours. Add more liquid if needed. Serve with noodles or mashed potatoes. *Serves 4.*

Edda Moser
was born in Berlin, and has sung regularly in Vienna, Salzburg, and Hamburg as well as at the Met, where she made her company debut in 1968. She writes, "My father was a musicologist, so I was very fortunate to grow up surrounded by some of the greatest musicians and scholars of our time. The one thing I learned was that no matter how much they argued about politics or music, they all agreed on good food. I have learned that anything can be resolved at the dinner table—provided the food is good!"

John Keenan
Veal Silviano

3 pounds boned shoulder of veal
¼ pound prosciutto, not too thinly sliced
2 large cloves garlic, minced
1 teaspoon chopped fresh rosemary
Freshly ground black pepper to taste
Salt to taste
2 tablespoons olive oil
2 tablespoons (¼ stick) butter
1 cup dry white wine, approximately

Preheat oven to 350 degrees. Lay the roast open on a flat surface, cover with sliced prosciutto, and sprinkle with garlic, rosemary, pepper, and salt. Tie the roast into a roll.

In a small, heatproof roasting pan, heat oil and butter, then brown the veal roll on all sides. Add ½ cup wine and bring to a boil. Cover pan loosely, place in oven, and cook until meat is cooked and soft, about 1½ to 2 hours. Turn the roast every 30 minutes and add more wine as needed to keep meat moist. *Serves 6.*

John Keenan
is the Assistant Chorus Master of the Met.

Otto Schenk
Viennese Beef Goulash

3 tablespoons oil, butter, or beef drippings
4 medium onions, thickly sliced
2 tablespoons Hungarian sweet paprika
1 tablespoon hot paprika
Salt to taste
1 chili pepper, minced (optional)
1 clove garlic, minced (optional)
2 pounds lean, tender beef cut from the loin, in
  1-inch cubes
1 cup beef broth

In a large, heavy pot or Dutch oven, heat oil and cook onions over low heat until golden, about 5 minutes; take care not to let them burn. Add paprikas, salt, chili pepper, and garlic; mix well, cover tightly, and steam for 5 minutes. Add beef, mix well, cover, and simmer very slowly until meat is done, about 1 hour. Moisten occasionally with a little broth, but most of the sauce will come from the meat and onions. Serve with salt sticks, black bread, or gnocchi and beer. *Serves 4 to 6.*

Note If any sauce is left over, use it to heat sausages and serve a Viennese favorite, *Wuerstl mit Saft.*

Otto Schenk
is famous as both an actor and an
opera director, and has staged eleven
operas at the Met, including
Fidelio, Tannhäuser, Les Contes
d'Hoffmann, *the company's new*
Ring, *and* Die Fledermaus, *in*
which he also appeared as the jailer.
He also loves to cook for his friends
at his country retreat.

ABOVE AND OPPOSITE: *Otto Schenk.*

Lily Pons and her husband, André Kostelanetz.

Lily Pons
Crepes de Boeuf

1 small onion, minced
2 tablespoons (¼ stick) butter or meat drippings
1 cup finely chopped cooked beef
¼ teaspoon salt
Dash of black pepper
1 cup sifted flour
1 egg, lightly beaten
1½ cups milk
Softened butter
Chopped fresh parsley

Brown onion in 1 tablespoon butter. Add meat, salt, and pepper, then stir and cook for 1 minute.

Place flour in a mixing bowl and add a dash of salt. Combine the egg and milk and beat into the flour. Melt the remaining butter and stir in. Add the meat mix-ture and blend. Cook as you would large pancakes. When done, spread with butter, sprinkle with parsley, and roll tightly. Serve piping hot. *Serves 4 to 6.*

Lily Pons (1898–1976) was one of the most popular artists ever to sing at the Met. She made her company debut as Lucia in 1931, and thereafter sang twenty-eight seasons in other coluratura roles, as well as in several films. Though she left the Met in 1958, she sang in concert into her seventies, still a glamorous personality.

Regina Resnik
Gala Cold Veal Roast

¼ cup vegetable oil (or half olive oil, half vegetable oil)

1 tablespoon white wine vinegar

1 tablespoon grated onion

1 teaspoon crushed rosemary leaves

1 teaspoon Dijon mustard

Salt and pepper to taste

3–4 pounds boned shoulder of veal, cut with a pocket

2 tablespoons (¼ stick) butter

¾ cup chopped onion

¾ cup finely chopped celery

⅓ cup chopped fresh parsley

1 cup diced pitted prunes

1 cup dried apricots, chopped

1 cup chopped walnuts

6–8 slices stale white bread, crusts removed, soaked in milk and squeezed dry

1 teaspoon tapioca

3–4 eggs

1 cup chicken broth or water

Combine the oil, vinegar, grated onion, rosemary, and mustard. Season with salt and pepper, and blend well. Coat the meat with the mixture and let stand, refrigerated, for several hours.

In a skillet, heat butter and sauté onion, celery, and parsley until soft, about 5 minutes; do not let brown. In a bowl, combine onion mixture with all remaining ingredients except eggs and broth. Add the eggs, 1 at a time, and stir until the stuffing has the consistency of thick cooked cereal.

Preheat oven to 325 degrees. Hold the pocket of the marinated roast open and fill with stuffing. Reserve any remaining marinade. With thread and skewers or sewing with needle and thread, close the opening of the roast. Reshape it into a round loaf, and tie it to hold its shape. Place in a roasting pan, add chicken broth or water, and roast until meat is soft, about 2½ to 3 hours. Baste frequently with remaining marinade and pan juices. Serve hot or cold, with a rémoulade sauce, raisin-studded rice, small pasta with mushrooms, or a red and green salad. *Serves 6 to 8.*

Regina Resnik first came to the Met in 1944, and since then has returned for thirty seasons, singing both soprano and mezzo roles. She has also staged opera, and toured the country and played on Broadway in the revival of Cabaret. She and her husband, the artist Arbit Blatas, live in New York City and Venice, and she is a member of the Board of Directors of the Metropolitan Opera Guild.

Anna Moffo
Ossobuco alla Moffo

1 cup flour

6 slices meaty veal shank, each 2½ to 3 inches
  thick

1 medium onion

1 medium carrot, peeled

1 celery stalk

2 cloves garlic

Zest of ½ lemon

Small bunch of parsley

3 fresh basil leaves, or ¼ teaspoon dried

¼ teaspoon dried marjoram

¼ teaspoon freshly ground black pepper

¼ teaspoon salt

1 (2-ounce) can flat anchovies, drained

1 large, ripe tomato, peeled and seeded; or 1 cup
  drained, canned Italian plum tomatoes

½ cup (1 stick) butter

1 cup dry white wine

2 cups chicken broth, approximately

2 tablespoons tomato paste

Spread the flour in a flat pan. Wash and dry the shank pieces well, then dredge them abundantly in flour. Set aside on a plate, not touching each other. Chop or process the onion, carrot, celery, garlic, lemon zest, parsley, basil, marjoram, pepper, salt, anchovies, and tomato.

In a large, deep skillet or heavy shallow saucepan, heat the butter and sauté the well-floured meat to brown gently on all sides. Remove meat and keep warm. Add half the processed vegetable mixture to the pan and sauté gently, stirring a few times, until the vegetables are wilted and the onion pieces translucent, about 4 minutes. Return meat to pan, add wine, cook over low heat for 5 minutes, then turn the meat and sauté for another minute or two. Add the broth, cover the pan, and simmer for about 2 hours. Turn the meat every half hour, being careful not to break up the pieces as they become soft.

When the veal starts to get tender, sprinkle the remaining half of the processed mixture over the meat, stir the tomato paste into the sauce, and add more broth if the sauce is too thick. Cover again and simmer for 10 more minutes. Remove the shanks carefully to a serving dish, and spoon some of the gravy over them. *Serves 6.*

ABOVE: *Anna Moffo.* OPPOSITE: *Nicolai Gedda and Fernando Corena in* L'Elisir d'Amore.

Anna Moffo
first came to the Met in 1959, and
since then has sung more than 130
performances of eighteen soprano
roles, including Violetta, Lucia,
Gilda, and Massenet's Manon. She
says: "This should be served with
risotto Milanese (saffron risotto),
but for that recipe you will have to
wait for volume two of this cook-
book. Extra gravy over the risotto is
mmmm . . . good.

"I made my official operatic debut
in Milano in 1957 in Madama
Butterfly. I am sure eating a lot of
ossobuco at this time contributed to
my success. It has been one of my
very special recipes ever since.
I guess I like to cook because I
like to eat. But I also love seeing the
enjoyment and contentment of all
those faces around the table—faces
which I hope are as contented as
when I sing—but who can see them
in a dark theater?"

P. Michael Nordberg
Beef Patties in Cream Sauce

Patties

¼ cup minced onion
3 tablespoons butter
1½ pounds ground beef sirloin
2 tablespoons (¼ stick) butter, softened
Salt and pepper to taste
Pinch of dried thyme
1 egg, well beaten
2 tablespoons fines herbes (parsley, chives,
   tarragon, and/or chervil)
2 tablespoons oil
½ cup flour

Sauce

¼ cup beef broth
⅔ cup heavy cream
Salt and pepper to taste

Sauté onion in 1 tablespoon butter until translucent and soft, about 3 minutes. Combine with meat, softened butter, salt and pepper, thyme, beaten egg, and *fines herbes*. Mix well and shape into thick patties.

In a skillet, heat oil and remaining butter. Dredge patties in flour. Brown the patties on both sides, but do not overcook. Remove patties to a hot serving dish and keep warm. Pour fat from the skillet, deglaze quickly with beef broth, then add the cream, and season with salt and pepper. Reduce sauce over fairly high heat until the gravy is thick, then spoon over patties and serve. *Serves 4 to 6.*

*P. Michael Nordberg
has worked for the Met as a call boy
and driver when the company has
visited Minneapolis on tour, and has
long invited company members to his
famous dinners. This was a dish
served to them in 1975.*

Robert Merrill
Vitello Tonnato

Veal

3 tablespoons butter
3–4 pounds boneless veal roast, tied
2 medium onions, sliced
2 carrots, peeled and sliced
3 sprigs parsley
1 large bay leaf
2 cloves garlic, sliced
2 whole cloves
4 cups boiling water, or 2 cups chicken broth and
   2 cups water

Tuna Sauce

2 (6½-ounce) cans tuna fish, drained
8 anchovy filets
½ cup fresh lemon juice
1 cup oil, including oil drained from the tuna
4 teaspoons capers

Heat butter in a heavy saucepan or Dutch oven, and brown the roast on all sides. Pour off all fat from pan, then add onions, carrots, parsley, bay leaf, garlic, and cloves. Pour boiling water over all, cover tightly, and cook over low heat until meat is tender, about 2 to 2½ hours. Drain off liquid and let the meat cool.

In a blender, purée tuna, anchovies, and lemon juice at low speed until smooth. With the blender still running, gradually add the oil until the mixture has the consistency of a thin mayonnaise. Turn off the blender, and mix capers into the tuna sauce.

To serve, slice cold veal very thin. Place slices in a shallow serving dish and pour the sauce over the meat. Cover and marinate in the refrigerator for 24 hours. *Serves 8 to 10 as a first course.*

*Robert Merrill
first sang at the Met in 1945, and soon became one of the most popular baritones to appear with the company, singing over 550 performances in the house, and another 200 or so on tour. This recipe is from his wife, Marion Merrill, who adds: "I do love cooking, and Bob and I both enjoy different kinds of food. We've been lucky enough to be able to travel so much, and to sample different kinds of cuisine. When we're abroad and find a dish we like I try to get the recipe and make it at home. I do Chinese cooking, Indian, Italian, Russian—anything we like!"*

Zinka Milanov and Robert Merrill at Sherry's.

Martti Talvela
Lampaanpotka
LEG OF LAMB À LA
ANNUKKA

1 small leg of lamb (about 6 pounds)
6 cloves garlic, approximately
1 lemon, cut in half
Salt and pepper to taste
¼ teaspoon powdered sage
1 cup each dried morels and chanterelles, or dried
*   porcini and Chinese black mushrooms*
2 cups dry red wine, approximately
2 tablespoons (¼ stick) butter
1 cup heavy cream

Preheat oven to 500 degrees. Wipe the lamb, trim surplus fat, then make several deep incisions. Push in the garlic cloves until they are buried in the meat. Rub the lamb with lemon, sprinkle with salt, pepper, and sage, and place in a shallow roasting pan. Sear meat in hot oven for 30 minutes.

Grind half the dried mushrooms to a powder in a food processor. Pour half of the wine and the ground mushrooms over the roast. Reduce oven heat to 200 degrees and cook for 2 hours, basting from time to time with more wine and pan juices.

Meanwhile, soak remaining mushrooms in lukewarm water. When soft, drain well and mince. Sauté mushrooms in butter over medium heat for 3 minutes.

When lamb is done, remove to a serving dish. Pour off the pan juices, skimming off all the fat, then blend juices with cream and sautéed mushrooms. Adjust seasoning to taste, and serve gravy in a sauceboat alongside the sliced lamb. *Serves 6 to 8.*

Martti Talvela
the Finnish bass, made his Met
debut in 1968, and has sung more
than a hundred performances with
the company. He is celebrated for his
portrayal of Boris Godunov, and has
also sung Gurnemanz and Hunding
with the company. This dish is
named for his wife, Annukka.

LEFT: *Cesare Siepi at Sherry's.* OPPOSITE: *Martti Talvela displays a salmon and leg of lamb.*

Risë Stevens
Veal Goulash

3 pounds veal from shank, cut into large cubes
Flour for dredging
2 tablespoons (¼ stick) butter
2 large onions, chopped
1 clove garlic, minced
2 tablespoons Hungarian sweet Paprika
1 tablespoon water
1 green bell pepper, seeded and cut into large
  pieces
1 (12-ounce) can whole tomatoes
1 bay leaf
1 cup chicken broth, approximately
Salt and pepper to taste
1 cup sour cream

Dredge the meat in flour. In a large saucepan, heat butter and sauté meat, searing it on all sides. Remove meat to a warm platter. In the same pan, sauté onions and garlic until soft and translucent, about 5 minutes. Add paprika and water (to keep paprika from turning bitter). Stir well, then return meat to pan, add green pepper, tomatoes, bay leaf, and about ½ cup chicken broth. Mix well, bring to a boil, then season with salt and pepper. Cover pan, lower heat, and cook until meat is tender, about 1 hour. Add a little more broth if needed to keep mixture moist. When meat is cooked, stir the sour cream into the pan and heat through; do not let mixture come to a boil, to avoid curdling the sour cream. Serve with noodles, spaëtzle, or rice. *Serves 6.*

Note If the gravy is too thin, add a tablespoon of flour diluted in a tablespoon of water, stir well, and simmer for 2 or 3 more minutes.

Risë Stevens
to many opera lovers will always be
Carmen. The New York-born
mezzo-soprano first sang at the Met
in 1938, and remained on the com-
pany's roster for twenty-three years.
She sang many other roles as well,
including Octavian, Cherubino,
Dalila, and Orlovsky, but it was as

Bizet's gypsy that she most fervently captured the public's imagination. Miss Stevens is still associated with the Met, not only as a member of the Board of Directors of the Guild, but as the Advisor to the Met's Young Artists Development Program.

Miss Stevens explains: "My greatest pleasure is coming home and cooking dinner. I cook all the time. On weekends, I love roasting and building an exciting menu for Sunday dinner. I'm not much for desserts—I only make main dishes. I love to think up things to do with vegetables, like puréeing, to make them taste different. But I cook by instinct; I rarely do a dish the same way twice. Cooking is wonderful therapy for me. Whenever I have time off—a vacation or holiday—I turn to the kitchen.

"I didn't really learn to cook from my mother. My mother-in-law taught me all my Hungarian dishes, like this veal goulash. My father, actually, was a very good cook, but when he cooked no one else was allowed in the kitchen. And that's the way I am too!"

BELOW: *Risë Stevens in the kitchen.* OVERLEAF: *Arturo Sergi in the "Eating" scene from* Aufstieg und Fall der Stadt Mahagonny.

Andrea Velis
Cypriot Pork and Cauliflower alla Loulla

Pork and Cauliflower
3 tablespoons vegetable oil
2 pounds lean boneless pork, cubed
1 head cauliflower, separated into florets
¾ cup dry red wine, approximately
2 teaspoons caraway seed
Salt and pepper to taste
1 cup chicken broth, approximately

Bulgur alla Andrea
2 tablespoons vegetable oil
1 tablespoon chopped onion
1 cup bulgur (cracked wheat)
2 cups chicken broth
Salt and pepper to taste

Preheat oven to 350 degrees. In a skillet, heat oil and brown the pork cubes; set aside. Brown the cauliflower in the same skillet, then place pork and cauliflower in a large casserole. Deglaze skillet with ½ cup wine, then add pan juices and caraway seed to the casserole. Season with salt and pepper and add enough chicken broth to barely cover the mixture. Cover tightly and bake for about 1½ hours. Add a bit more wine if needed to keep moist. Do not stir while baking; shake casserole a few times, so as not to break up the cauliflower.

While pork and cauliflower cook, prepare bulgur. In a skillet, heat oil and sauté onion until golden and soft, about 5 minutes. Add bulgur and sauté, stirring often, until nicely browned. Gradually add broth, stir, and bring to a boil. Turn off heat. Cover tightly and let stand for about 15 minutes, or until all the broth is absorbed. Fluff with a fork before serving, and then top with the meat mixture. Serves 4 to 6.

*Andrea Velis
has been one of the Met's most
versatile performers, having sung
over 1,500 performances of over fifty
roles with the company, including
the Simpleton in Boris Godunov
and the Witch in Hansel and
Gretel.*

Martina Arroyo
Veal, Tomato, and Orange Stew

2 tablespoons (¼ stick) butter
2 tablespoons vegetable oil
1 large onion, sliced
3 cloves garlic
3 pounds stewing veal, cut into bite-size pieces
1 cup flour
1 scant tablespoon dried oregano

Freshly ground black pepper to taste
2 cups chicken broth
1 (32-ounce) can peeled tomatoes
1 pound fresh mushrooms
24 pickling (small white pearl) onions
Grated zest of 1 orange
Salt to taste

In a heavy saucepan, heat butter and oil. Add onion and garlic, and sauté, stirring a few times, until onion is golden brown, about 10 minutes. Dredge meat lightly in flour, add to the pan, and sauté while stirring until meat is lightly browned, about 10 minutes. Add oregano, season with pepper, then add chicken broth and stir until well blended. Add the tomatoes, bring to a boil, then cover and cook over low heat until meat is tender, about 1½ hours. When meat is nearly done, add the mushrooms, sliced, quartered, or left whole, depending on their size. Also add the pickling onions (if you use frozen ones, defrost before using), the orange zest, and salt. (Don't add the salt earlier, as the meat may get hard.) Serve with rice or buttered parslied potatoes, green peas, or a green salad. *Serves 6 to 8.*

Martina Arroyo
is a native New Yorker, and has
sung at the Met since 1959. She has sung

over 170 performances with the company,
most often as Leonore in both Trovatore
and Forza, *and as* Aida.

Alton E. Peters
Oxtail Stew

2 meaty oxtails, cut into 3-inch pieces (about
  3–4 pounds total)
1 cup flour
3 tablespoons oil
2 carrots, peeled and cut in rounds
2 medium onions, sliced
1 cup beef broth
1 (8-ounce) can stewed tomatoes
1 tablespoon tomato paste
¼ pound fresh mushrooms, sliced
½ teaspoon dried marjoram
Salt and pepper to taste
1 tablespoon Major Grey's chutney

Preheat oven to 250 degrees. Dredge oxtails in flour. In a heavy skillet, heat oil and brown oxtail pieces on all sides. Transfer them to a casserole. Brown carrots and onions in the same skillet, then add to the oxtails. Add all remaining ingredients, mix, and bring to a boil. Cover tightly and bake until meat is tender, about 3 to 3½ hours. This is best made the day ahead, then refrigerated. Before reheating, remove and discard fat from surface. *Serves 4.*

Inge Borkh
Savory Veal in Cream Sauce

2 green bell peppers
2 red bell peppers
4 large onions
¼ cup vegetable oil
3 tablespoons butter
2 pounds boneless veal shoulder, cut into thin strips
1 tablespoon Hungarian sweet paprika
Cayenne pepper or Tabasco to taste
½ teaspoon curry powder, or to taste
Salt and pepper to taste
⅔ cup heavy cream

Seed the peppers, and cut into very thin strips. Slice the onions very thin. In a deep skillet, heat 2 tablespoons oil, then sauté the pepper strips over gentle heat until very soft, about 5 minutes; stir often. Remove and reserve the peppers. Add remaining oil to skillet, and sauté the sliced onions until very soft, translucent, and just starting to take on color, about 5 minutes. Remove onions and reserve.

Discard oil in the skillet, then add the butter. Sauté the veal strips over medium heat until veal is tender, about 10 to 15 minutes. Stir and turn while cooking. Return peppers and onions to pan, mix gently, then stir in paprika, cayenne, and curry. Season with salt and pepper, and heat through. Stir in the cream and simmer for another minute, then serve with potato puree or noodles. *Serves 4.*

Inge Borkh
was born in Mannheim, Germany. She has appeared at the Met as Salome and Elektra. "This is one of my very favorite dishes. The little additional work in slicing the vegetables very thin is well worth it—the result is delicious."

Edward Johnson at the barbeque pit.

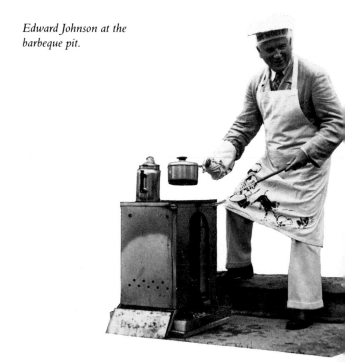

Paolo Montarsolo
Saltimbocca alla Romana

12 veal scallops (about 2¼ pounds total)
12 slices prosciutto
12 sage leaves
Salt to taste
½ cup flour
¼ cup (½ stick) butter, plus 1 teaspoon for sauce
Freshly ground black pepper
¾ cup dry white wine
½ cup beef broth

Flatten the veal scallops with a cleaver or heavy weight. Lay a slice of prosciutto and a sage leaf (or a pinch of dried sage) on each slice of veal. Season lightly with salt. Fold and secure with a toothpick. Dredge rolls in flour.

In a skillet, heat butter and add the scallops. Sauté quickly on each side until browned, about 2 minutes. Season with salt and pepper, then add ½ cup wine. Reduce wine by one-half over high heat. Remove veal to a warm serving dish, and remove toothpicks. Deglaze skillet with remaining wine and beef broth. Reduce sauce to half its volume, swirl in a teaspoon of butter, spoon sauce over veal, and serve. *Serves 6.*

Paolo Montarsolo
made his Met debut as Don
Pasquale in 1975, and has since
returned to sing bass roles in Il
Barbiere di Siviglia, Le Nozze di
Figaro, *and* L'Italiana in Algeri.
He lives in Rome.

Leonie Rysanek
Party Veal

8 thin slices veal (about 1½ pounds total)
Salt and pepper to taste
2 tablespoons flour
2 tablespoons (¼ stick) butter
½ pound fresh mushrooms, sliced
2 tablespoons chopped drained capers
2 tablespoons minced fresh parsley
1 cup sour cream

Trim any gristle or fat from veal, then lightly pound the slices. Sprinkle with salt and pepper, then dredge lightly with 1 tablespoon flour. In a skillet, heat butter and brown the veal on both sides. Remove to a serving platter and keep warm.

Add mushrooms, capers, and parsley to the skillet, and sauté until the mushrooms give up their juice. Remove mushrooms with a slotted spoon and arrange on top of the veal. Beat sour cream with remaining flour, add mixture to the pan juices, mix well, and heat while stirring until the sauce thickens. Spoon over veal and serve at once. *Serves 4.*

José van Dam
Pork Hocks à la Belge

2 fresh pork hocks (knuckles)
1 pound Brussels sprouts, trimmed
1 pound carrots, peeled and each cut into 4 pieces
3 leeks (white parts only), washed and each cut into 4 pieces
2 small onions, peeled
4 cloves garlic
1 whole clove
Pinch of dried thyme
1 bay leaf
Salt and pepper to taste
6 white turnips, peeled and halved

Place meat and all other ingredients except turnips in a large saucepan. Cover with water and bring to a boil. Reduce heat, cover, and simmer until meat is cooked and separates easily from the bone, about 1 to 1½ hours. About 15 minutes before the meat is done, add the turnips. Serve hot with the broth, accompanied by boiled potatoes. *Serves 4.*

*José van Dam
has sung the roles of Escamillo, the Dutchman, Wozzeck, Figaro, and Jochanaan at the Met since his company debut in 1975. He lives in his native Belgium.*

Joyce Rasmussen Balint
Spareribs and Brown Cabbage

1 large, firm head green cabbage
3 tablespoons sugar
3 tablespoons butter
½ cup water
Salt and pepper to taste
2 pounds country-style spareribs

Remove outer leaves and core cabbage. Shred the cabbage coarsely. In a large saucepan, brown the sugar until caramel colored; do not let it scorch. Add butter, and stir constantly over low heat for about 4 minutes. Add shredded cabbage. Stir and mix with a wooden spoon to brown the cabbage. Add water, mix, cover tightly, and simmer for about 1 hour. Stir occasionally. Season with salt and pepper.

Add spareribs and a little more water, if needed, to prevent sticking. Stir a few times and cook until meat is tender, about 1 more hour. *Serves 4.*

*Joyce Rasmussen Balint
is a mandolinist with the Met Orchestra, and is married to Sandor Balint, a violinist in the orchestra.*

Phyllis Curtin
Mandarin Ham Slices

4 slices cooked ham (baked or roasted), about ½
inch thick
Whole cloves
Ground ginger
4 teaspoons dark brown sugar
1 teaspoon grated orange zest
½ cup Champagne or sparkling white wine
1 cup canned Mandarin oranges, with juice

Preheat oven to 350 degrees. Trim fat from ham and make incisions to insert cloves in each slice. Sprinkle each slice with a pinch of ginger, a teaspoon of brown sugar, and a little of the grated orange zest. Arrange slices in a lightly greased baking dish and bake for 10 minutes. Drain off liquid.

Combine Champagne and juice from oranges and carefully pour around slices so as not to disturb sugar and seasonings. Lower heat to 300 degrees and bake 15 minutes longer, basting frequently. Add more juice or Champagne if needed. Remove cloves and serve each slice garnished with orange sections and some of the sauce. *Serves 4.*

Phyllis Curtin
was born in West Virginia, and sang
at the New York City Opera before
making her Met debut in 1961. She
sang a number of important soprano
roles with the company, including
Donna Anna, Rosalinda, Fiordiligi,
Ellen Orford, and Violetta.

Phyllis Curtin.

Dorothy Kirsten
Braised Lamb Shanks

3 tablespoons flour
Salt and pepper to taste
Paprika to taste
4 lamb shanks (about 4 pounds)
2 tablespoons (¼ stick) butter
2 tablespoons oil
1 large onion, very thinly sliced
1 cup dry red wine
1¼ cups water
Pinch of rosemary leaves
1 bay leaf
2 tablespoons minced fresh parsley
Mint jelly

Preheat oven to 350 degrees. Season half the flour with salt, pepper, and paprika. Trim lamb shanks, remove excess fat, and lightly dust shanks with seasoned flour. In a large saucepan or Dutch oven, heat butter and oil. Sauté the shanks until well browned on all sides, then remove to a plate. Add sliced onion to pan and sauté over medium heat until lightly browned, about 2 minutes. Return meat to pan, add wine, 1 cup water, rosemary, and bay leaf.

Cover and bake until meat is easily pierced with a fork, about 2 hours. Remove the shanks and keep hot.

Mix remaining flour with remaining ¼ cup water and add to the pan juices. Blend and cook, while stirring, until gravy comes to a boil. Reduce heat and simmer until thickened to right consistency. Strain the gravy, if desired. Garnish shanks with minced parsley, and serve gravy on the side. And mint jelly, of course. *Serves 4 to 6.*

Dorothy Kirsten first graced the Met stage in 1945, and for twenty-seven seasons sang 165 performances of roles such as Butterfly, Tosca, Violetta, and Mimi. She has also had an extensive radio and television career, and appeared in several films. Miss Kirsten now lives in Santa Barbara, California.

She says, "In my youth I never had much interest in cooking—I was too busy having fun and enjoying sports. My husband, Jack, also loved sports, and when we married I also discovered he liked to cook.

"When I was not touring we would escape to our country home and after a round of golf, sharing the kitchen became a pleasure. Jack was a wiz with the barbecue, and I would dream up exotic salads and steamed vegetables. One of his favorite dishes was my baked lamb shanks; it was a special favorite of our golfing pals, too."

OPPOSITE: *Dorothy Kirsten.*

Zachary Solov
Boiled Tongue with Raisin Sauce

Tongue
1 smoked beef tongue (4–5 pounds)
1 medium onion
3 cloves garlic
2 bay leaves
6 black peppercorns

Raisin Sauce
2 tablespoons vegetable oil
1 medium onion, diced
2 tablespoons flour
2 tablespoons currant jelly
⅓ cup vinegar
⅓ cup honey
½ teaspoon ground ginger
½ teaspoon salt
¼ cup seedless raisins
¼ cup slivered almonds
1 lemon, thinly sliced

Rinse the tongue in cold water. Place in a deep kettle, add other ingredients, and cover with cold water. Bring to a boil, reduce heat, and simmer for about 3 hours. Add more boiling water if needed to keep up level. When the tongue is cooked, let it cool in the stock just enough to remove skin and trim the thick end. Reserve 2 cups of the stock for the sauce.

In a saucepan, heat oil and lightly brown the onion. Sprinkle flour on the browned onion, and gradually add the reserved tongue stock, stirring, until the mixture boils and is smooth. Stir in currant jelly, vinegar, honey, ginger, salt, and raisins. Simmer for 5 minutes. Add almonds and lemon slices and simmer for 3 more minutes. Slice tongue and serve with the sauce. *Serves 6.*

Zachary Solov is a choreographer who has been associated with the Met since 1951. His ballets have been seen in productions of Aida, La Gioconda, Faust, *and the current production of* Samson et Dalila. *He notes that "Potato pancakes go well with this dinner, with a sour cream topping and tart applesauce. Have fun!"*

Helen Traubel
Boiled Beef Tongue with Polish Sauce

1 fresh beef tongue (4–5 pounds)
¼ pound ground veal
¼ pound ground pork
1 large calves brain
2 tablespoons (¼ stick) butter
1 tablespoon flour
Salt and pepper

Grace Moore in the 1937 film The King Steps Out.

6 gingersnaps, crumbled

3 thin slices lemon

¼ cup dried currants or raisins

2–3 tablespoons distilled white vinegar
   (optional)

12 blanched almonds, finely chopped

Place beef tongue in a pot with salted hot water and boil until tender, about 1½ to 2 hours. When done, take out of water. When cool enough to handle, peel outside skin from tongue, trim thick end, and slice tongue thin. Save broth.

Prepare meatballs by mixing together veal and pork. Roll into small balls about as round as a quarter, place in boiling salted water to boil slowly for about 5 minutes. Then remove from broth, and save broth. Set meatballs aside.

Prepare brains by cleaning carefully, taking off the outside skin. Cut in small pieces and let stand in hot water for 5 minutes. Set aside.

To prepare sauce, melt butter in a large frying pan or pot, then add flour, stirring constantly until browned; ladle in enough broth from cooking tongue and meatballs to reach desired thickness (approximately 3 to 4 cups of broth). Add salt and pepper to taste, then stir in gingersnaps, lemon slices, currants or raisins, and vinegar, if desired. Just before serving, add almonds, meatballs, brains, and tongue to the sauce. Simmer gently for a few minutes, then serve. *Serves 6 to 8.*

Helen Traubel (1899–1972) was one of the finest American Wagnerian sopranos. She sang the great German roles at the Met from 1937 into the 1950s, and thereafter pursued a career in nightclubs, television, and on Broadway.

Eva Marton

Marton Family's Layered Cabbage

1 large onion, chopped fine
2 tablespoons lard or bacon drippings
1 pound lean ground pork
1 pound lean ground beef
1 clove garlic, minced
1 tablespoon Hungarian sweet paprika, plus
    additional for baking
2 pounds sauerkraut
1 cup cooked white rice
3 tablespoons sour cream

In a heavy skillet, sauté onion in 1 tablespoon fat over low heat until onion is translucent and soft, about 10 minutes. Stir a few times. Add pork, beef, garlic, and paprika, and mix well. Cook mixture over very low heat for another 10 to 15 minutes.

Preheat oven to 350 degrees. Place sauerkraut in a saucepan, bring to a boil, then drain. Grease a large heatproof casserole with remaining fat. Place a layer of half the sauerkraut on the bottom of the casserole, followed by a layer of half the meat mixture, then a layer of all the rice, and a layer of the remaining meat. Top with the remaining sauerkraut.

Bake for 30 minutes, then spread sour cream on top, sprinkle with additional paprika, and reduce oven to 300 degrees. Bake for another 30 minutes, then serve. *Serves 6.*

Zinka Milanov

Djuveč

10 medium onions, finely chopped
10 large tomatoes, sliced
½ cup white rice, rinsed
7 potatoes, peeled and sliced
5 lamb chops (about 1 pound)
5 pork chops (about 1½ pounds)
6 green bell peppers, cored and seeded
1 eggplant, peeled and diced
1 cup drained canned okra
Salt and pepper to taste
2 tablespoons (¼ stick) butter, in pieces

Preheat oven to 400 degrees. Spread onions on the bottom of a large roasting pan. Arrange a layer of tomato slices on the onions. Sprinkle rice over tomatoes. Add a layer of sliced potatoes. Add chops, alternating lamb and pork. Slice peppers into rings, then cover chops with eggplant cubes and pepper rings. Add a second layer of sliced tomatoes. Top with okra. Sprinkle with salt and pepper, then dot with butter. Cover and roast until meat is tender, about 1 hour. Remove cover, and brown top for 15 minutes. *Serves 8 to 10.*

*Zinka Milanov
was born in Zagreb, Croatia. She
was a favorite at the Met for twenty-
four seasons, in which she sang such
roles as Aida, Gioconda, both
Leonoras, and Amelia. She lives in
New York City, teaches singing,
and is well known in operatic circles
for her culinary talents.*

Fedora Barbieri
Braised Meat Loaf

1 pound ground veal
1 pound ground lean pork
2 eggs, lightly beaten
2 cloves garlic, minced
3 tablespoons minced fresh parsley
¼ pound grated Parmesan cheese
Salt and pepper to taste
2 large carrots, peeled
2 Italian sausages, removed from casing
  (optional)
2 hard-boiled eggs
½ cup flour
½ cup fine dry bread crumbs
¼ cup olive oil
3 tablespoons butter
½ cup dry white wine, approximately

Mix veal and pork with beaten eggs, garlic, parsley, and Parmesan. Season with salt and pepper, then let stand for 15 minutes. In the meantime, cook the carrots in boiling water until just soft, about 15 minutes.

Spread the meat mixture in a rectangle on a sheet of wax paper. Spread the sausage meat (if desired) in the center of the rectangle, place the 2 carrots lengthwise on top, and add the hard-boiled eggs. Lift the edge of the wax paper and shape the meat into a roll. Mix the flour and bread crumbs, and roll the loaf in mixture until it is well covered.

In a deep skillet or rectangular pan, heat oil and butter. Transfer the meat roll carefully to the pan and sauté for about 10 to 15 minutes, turning the roll very gently until well browned on all sides. Add the wine, cover the pan, and cook over very low heat for about 30 minutes. Add more wine as needed and baste a few times with pan juices. Transfer loaf carefully to a serving dish, and let rest for 15 minutes. Serve with pan gravy. *Serves 6.*

*Fedora Barbieri
made her Met debut as Eboli in
Don Carlo in 1950. She has appeared as a leading mezzo-soprano
in opera houses all over the world,
including La Scala, Covent Garden,
San Francisco, the Verona Arena,
and the Colón, Buenos Aires. She
now lives in Florence.*

Mother's Plantation Shortbread
Osie Hawkins

Chicken Figaro
Richard Bonelli

Hungarian Chicken Paprikás with Dumplings
Frank T. Kamenar

Chicken Vermouth
Barbara Daniels

Chicken and Vegetables Turandot
James S. Marcus

Pollo alla *Pirata*
Elaine B. Kones

Baked Chicken
Isola Jones

Chicken Tandoori
John W. Freeman

Chicken Tetrazzini

Chicken Elisabetta
Elisabeth Rethberg

Suprême of Chicken Rossini

Chicken Casserole
Lawrence Tibbett

Chicken in Pomegranate-Walnut Sauce
Mrs. Ezra K. Zilkha

Mother's Curried Chicken
Erin Langston

Cassoulet Bakal
Shirley Bakal

Křepelky Pečené
Yveta Synek Graff

Alföldi Paprikás Pulyka
Sándor Kónya

Holoubata s Nádivkou
Yveta Synek Graff

OPPOSITE: *Lawrence Tibbett holds his prize hens, Tabitha and Mehitabel.* OVERLEAF: *Chicken Tetrazzini, with a photo of Madame Tetrazzini, the veil she wore in* Lucia di Lammermoor, *and Gioachino Rossini's cane handle.*

POULTRY AND GAME

Osie Hawkins
Mother's Plantation Shortbread

Cornbread

1 cup yellow cornmeal
1 cup self-rising flour, or 1 cup all-purpose flour
  mixed with 1 teaspoon baking powder
½ teaspoon sugar
½ teaspoon salt
¼ cup vegetable shortening or oil
1 egg
1 cup milk

White Sauce

3 tablespoons butter
3 tablespoons flour
2½ cups milk
Dash of cayenne pepper
Salt and pepper to taste

Filling

1½ cups diced cooked chicken or turkey
1½ cups diced cooked ham
1 cup cooked green peas; or 1 (8½-ounce) can,
  drained
1 (4-ounce) jar pimientos, drained and chopped

Preheat oven to 425 degrees. Generously grease an 8-inch square baking pan about 2 inches deep. Blend ingredients for cornbread, then pour mixture into prepared pan and bake until nicely browned, 20 to 30 minutes.

In a saucepan, melt butter for sauce. Stir in flour until smooth, then add milk and seasonings, stirring over low heat until smooth and thickened. Add the filling ingredients, and simmer to heat through.

Remove cornbread from pan. Cut into squares. Slice horizontally through each square. Place 1 bottom half on each serving plate, spoon the sauce mixture over it, top with other slice of cornbread, and spoon a generous amount of sauce over. Serves 4 to 6.

*Osie Hawkins
sang baritone roles at the Met for
twenty-three seasons, and thereafter
was for many years the company's
Executive Stage Manager.*

OPPOSITE: *Anna Moffo.*

Richard Bonelli
Chicken Figaro

6 tablespoons (¾ stick) butter
1 onion, thinly sliced
4 broiling chickens, split in half
1 pint heavy cream
2 cups fresh mushroom caps
1 cup brandy
1 teaspoon curry powder
Salt and pepper

Preheat oven to 325 degrees. Heat ¼ cup of the butter in a heavy skillet and sauté the onion until golden, about 3 minutes. Add the chicken and sauté over low heat until chicken is a delicate, even brown, about 5 minutes. Transfer to a self-basting roasting pan, dot with remaining butter, and pour the cream over. Place the mushroom caps on the chicken and cover the pan. Allow the chicken to steam in slow oven for 1 hour, basting every 15 minutes. About 15 minutes before the chicken is done, add the brandy and baste the meat well with this sauce.

Remove the chicken and mushrooms to a hot platter, then add the curry powder to the cream sauce, stirring well so that the cream, brandy, and curry are well blended. Add salt and pepper to taste, then pour sauce over the chicken and mushrooms. This dish is delicious served on a bed of wild rice. *Serves 8.*

Richard Bonelli (1887–1980) was a leading baritone at the Met during the 1930s and '40s. Born in Port Bryon, New York, he sang over a hundred performances with the company.

Frank T. Kamenar
Hungarian Chicken Paprikás with Dumplings

Chicken

⅓ cup butter
1 cup chopped onions
1 tablespoon Hungarian sweet paprika
Salt and pepper to taste
4 pounds chicken pieces
1 cup chicken broth
1 cup sour cream

Dumplings

2 eggs
2 cups flour
½ cup water

In a saucepan, heat butter and sauté onions until they just begin to take color, about 3 minutes. Add paprika, salt, and pepper; stir, then add chicken and broth. Cover and simmer until chicken is done, about 1 hour.

Mix and blend dumpling ingredients

with a fork until the batter is smooth. Let stand until cold water in a kettle or large pan comes to a boil. Cut dough into teaspoonful bits and drop the pieces into lightly salted boiling water. Cook for 5 minutes, then drain well.

Remove chicken to serving dish and keep hot. Stir sour cream into the hot sauce (do not let boil), then mix well and pour sauce over the chicken. Serve with dumplings. *Serves 6 to 8.*

Frank T. Kamenar
is the Director of Finance at the
Met. This recipe was contributed by
his mother, Goldie.

Barbara Daniels
Chicken Vermouth

4 whole chicken breasts, skinned, boned, and cut in half
2 cloves garlic, slivered
Ground cinnamon
2 tablespoons (¼ stick) butter, approximately
¾ cup chopped onions
1 cup sliced or chopped fresh mushrooms
¾ cup sliced pimento-stuffed olives
½ cup dry vermouth
½ cup heavy cream
Salt and pepper to taste

Flatten the halved breasts slightly. Place garlic slivers on each half, then sprinkle with a little cinnamon. Roll up the pieces, cover, and chill for 1 hour or more.

In a skillet, heat butter and sauté onions until glossy, about 5 minutes. Add mushrooms and sauté for a few minutes, then add olives and cook for another minute or two. Remove mixture to bowl. Add more butter to the skillet if needed, and sauté chicken pieces until nicely browned on all sides, about 5 minutes; do not overcook. Return onion-mushroom mixture to the skillet, add vermouth, stir, and bring to a boil. Stir in the cream and season with salt and pepper. Reduce heat, cover the skillet, and simmer for 10 minutes. Remove from heat and let stand, covered, for 10 minutes before serving. Serve with brown or white rice. *Serves 4.*

Note To "jazz up" this dish, add a sprinkling of curry and ginger to the cinnamon.

Barbara Daniels
has sung at Covent Garden, the
Paris Opera, and in the United
States with the Houston, Washing-
ton, and San Francisco Opera com-
panies. She made her Met debut in
1983, and has sung Musetta and
Violetta with the company.

James S. Marcus
Chicken and Vegetables Turandot

A CULINARY RENDITION
OF ACT II, SCENE 2
Riddle One:
What are the ingredients?

Answer:
HOPE plus the following:

1 large Spanish onion
¾ cup water
1 pound boned chicken breast
12 ounces fresh bean sprouts (do not use canned)
Garlic powder
Japanese soy sauce
About 15 fresh medium mushrooms, sliced
6 ounces fresh snow peas, trimmed

Riddle Two:
How are the ingredients blended?

Answer:
Without BLOOD, Sweat, and Tears:

Slice onion into 6 or 7 pieces and place in 4-quart Dutch oven. Add water and cook over high heat until onion separates into rings and water evaporates, about 5 minutes.

Simultaneously, cut chicken into bite-size pieces and place in saucepan coated with nonstick-spray. Cook chicken over high heat, stirring rapidly with wooden spoon until chicken becomes white on outside, about 2 to 3 minutes. (Do not brown chicken.) Set aside.

Drain Dutch oven if any water is left. Add bean sprouts, sprinkle liberally with garlic powder, and soak with soy sauce.

Cook for about 1½ minutes, stirring, until bean sprouts begin to soften.

Add chicken pieces and stir. Add mushrooms and stir for about 2 minutes.

Add snow peas, cover, and cook until pea pods become bright green, about 1½ minutes. Do not overcook; peas should be crunchy.

Stir pot and drain contents.

Riddle Three:
How many can be served?

Answer:
TURANDOT plus:

Calaf and Liu, no matter how ample they are. If Ping, Pang, and Pong amble by, serve with rice or noodles or double the quantities. Freshly prepared Colman's dry mustard is an excellent condiment. (One teaspoon per diner is more than sufficient.)

While this recipe is not to lose one's head over, it is delicious, nutritious, low-calorie, almost cholesterol-free, and easy to prepare in less than 30 minutes. Leftovers can be drained, refrigerated, and reheated in a microwave oven. Unlike a performance of *Turandot*, not as good the second time.

*James S. Marcus
is Chairman of the Board of the
Metropolitan Opera Association,
and a member of the Board of
Directors of the Metropolitan Opera
Guild.*

Elaine B. Kones
Pollo alla Pirata

½ cup flour
1 teaspoon salt
½ teaspoon freshly ground black pepper
1 teaspoon dried oregano
1 teaspoon dried basil
1 roasting chicken (about 3 pounds), cut up
¼ cup olive oil
¼ cup (½ stick) butter
1 cup dry white wine or dry vermouth
2 cups canned tomatoes, with juice
2 cloves garlic, minced
1 small onion, minced
1 teaspoon Tabasco

10 fresh medium mushrooms, sliced
6 black peppercorns, cracked
1 bay leaf
2 tablespoons chopped fresh parsley

Preheat oven to 350 degrees. Mix flour, salt, pepper, oregano, and basil. Dredge chicken pieces in the mixture. Reserve the remaining seasoned flour.

In a large skillet, heat oil and butter. Brown the chicken on all sides, then remove the chicken and place in a heavy casserole. To the remaining fat in the skillet add the reserved flour mixture, blend, then stir in the wine with a wire whisk. Whisk until the sauce is smooth and thickened; add a little more wine if the sauce is too thick. Pour the sauce over the chicken.

Remove skillet from heat, add all other ingredients except the parsley, stir gently, and deglaze the skillet. Spoon the mixture over the chicken. Cover the casserole with a heavy lid, and bake until chicken is tender, about 45 minutes. Garnish with chopped parsley and serve with cooked noodles or rice. *Serves 4.*

Isola Jones
Baked Chicken

¼ cup (½ stick) butter
1 chicken (about 3 pounds), cut up
2 teaspoons Hungarian sweet paprika
1 small head green cabbage (½ pound), cored and
    sliced ½ inch thick
Salt and pepper to taste
2 red cooking apples, peeled, cored, and sliced
1 medium onion, thinly sliced
1 teaspoon grated lemon zest
2 teaspoons caraway seed
1 teaspoon sugar
1½ cups grated Swiss cheese

In a large skillet, melt butter. Brown chicken pieces on all sides over medium heat. Dust with paprika, then cover the skillet tightly and cook over low heat for 30 minutes. Turn once during cooking. If needed, add a few spoonfuls of water to keep moist.

In the meantime, preheat oven to 350 degrees. Place sliced cabbage in a buttered 9 × 13-inch baking dish. Season with salt and pepper; cover dish with aluminum foil. Bake until almost tender, about 20 minutes. Remove from oven.

Arrange apples and onion on top of the cabbage, then sprinkle with lemon zest, caraway, and sugar. Place chicken pieces on top. Cover again with foil and bake until cabbage and chicken are cooked, about another 25 to 30 minutes. Remove from oven, uncover, and sprinkle with cheese. Return to oven just until the cheese is melted, 2 to 3 minutes. *Serves 4.*

*Isola Jones
made her Met debut in 1977, and
has since sung Carmen, Lola in
Cavalleria Rusticana, Giulietta in
Les Contes d'Hoffmann,
Maddalena in Rigoletto, and the
Strawberry Woman in Porgy and Bess.*

John W. Freeman
Chicken Tandoori

2 broilers, split in half
1½ pints plain yogurt
1½ tablespoons lemon or lime juice
1½ tablespoons butter, melted
1 clove garlic, crushed
1 tablespoon curry powder
⅛ teaspoon ground ginger

With a sharp knife, make little slits in the chicken. Place chicken in a bowl. Blend all other ingredients, pour over chicken, and marinate in refrigerator for several hours.

Heat broiler, then broil chicken for about 20 minutes on each side until done; baste often with marinade. Serve with plain brown or white rice. *Serves 4.*

OPPOSITE: *Isola Jones as the Strawberry Woman in* Porgy and Bess.

Chicken Tetrazzini

2 chickens (about 2 pounds each), quartered
½ pound fresh mushrooms, thinly sliced
5 tablespoons butter
3 tablespoons flour
1¼ cups heavy cream
¼ cup dry sherry
Pinch of grated nutmeg
Salt and pepper to taste
1 pound spaghetti
½ cup grated Parmesan cheese

Place chicken in a large pot, cover with boiling water, and simmer until tender, about 45 minutes. Remove chicken from pot. Skin and remove all bones, then cut the meat into small, thin strips. Return skin and bones to the pan and cook rapidly until broth is reduced to about 2½ cups, about 10 minutes. Strain the broth and skim the fat.

Sauté the mushrooms in 2 tablespoons butter until they just start to take on color, about 3 minutes. Remove from heat and reserve.

In a small saucepan, melt remaining butter, combine with flour, and blend well. Stir over low heat for a minute, then, while stirring, gradually add the hot chicken broth; blend until free of lumps and thickened. Add cream and sherry and stir until smooth. Season with nutmeg, salt, and pepper, then remove from heat.

Preheat oven to 350 degrees. Cook spaghetti until *al dente*, and drain well. Combine spaghetti with the mushrooms and mix with half the cream sauce. Mix the other half with the shredded chicken. Place spaghetti in a large baking dish. Make a hollow in the center and spoon in the chicken. Sprinkle with grated cheese and bake until lightly browned, about 10 to 15 minutes. *Serves 6.*

Chicken Tetrazzini was named after the famous Italian soprano Luisa Tetrazzini (1871–1940). She sang only eight performances at the Met during the 1911–12 season, but was one of the most famous singers of her day. A well-known gourmand and a great celebrity of the early twentieth century, she inspired this dish, as well as Noodles Tetrazzini and others.

TETRAZZINI IS NOW REPENTING

Ate Boston Beans, Brown Bread and Sardines, and Can't Sail.

Mme Luisa Tetrazzini is a victim of Boston baked beans and Boston brown bread, and she is ill in her apartments in the Knickerbocker Hotel. Her digestion, which she is proud to say has assimilated every European dish, fell down before Boston beans and Boston bread on Sunday morning, and as a result she had to delay her trip to Europe.

She was booked to sail this morning on the Mauretania to open the opera season at Covent Garden in London in "La Traviata" on April 26. But at the last moment Signor Bazelli, her manager, cancelled the passage. Mme Tetrazzini, who is as robust as most prima donnas, had often told her friends that she could eat anything, and some of them told her to beware of Boston. She laughed. After a breakfast of beans and brown bread she ate a box of sardines later in the day. While she might have been able to handle the beans and the bread, her stomach rebelled when the sardines came along. So when she came back to New York she had developed a case of acute gastritis. Dr. Ludwig Lang was called in just in time. Two trained nurses were sent for. They spent last night in her apartments at the hotel and were with her to-day.

"She is resting easily," said the doctor this afternoon. "She may be able to sail Saturday. I shall be at her bedside to-night unless she improves."

But at the Manhattan Opera House, and at the pier from which the Mauretania sailed other singers, there were various rumors about the prima donna's sickness. Some of the singers had it that the operation for an abscess had been performed on her ear. At the opera house it was ____ that she had been troubled ____

To Mr. Howard. E. Potter, from Luisa Tetrazzini. Baltimore 1920

Elisabeth Rethberg
Chicken Elisabetta

3 tablespoons butter
3 tablespoons vegetable oil
1 frying chicken (about 3 pounds), cut into
  serving pieces
¾ cup flour, approximately, seasoned with
  cayenne pepper, salt, and black pepper
Juice of 1 lemon
3 cloves garlic, minced
2 teaspoons crushed rosemary leaves
¼ cup soy sauce, approximately
1 cup dry sherry

Preheat oven to 350 degrees. In a heavy, ovenproof skillet or pan, heat butter and oil. Dredge chicken pieces in seasoned flour (or shake them in a bag). Brown the chicken, skin side first, in skillet. While browning, sprinkle chicken with lemon juice. When browned, sprinkle garlic and rosemary over the chicken and brush each piece with soy sauce. Turn the pieces, remove from heat, cover the skillet, and let stand for 3 or 4 minutes until you smell the garlic. Add ¾ cup sherry to skillet, cover again, and bake for 45 minutes. Remove cover and bake another 15 minutes. Add more sherry if needed to keep chicken moist. *Serves 4.*

Elisabeth Rethberg (1894–1976) sang in Dresden and Salzburg before coming to the Met in 1922, and remained with the company for twenty consecutive seasons. She sang 270 performances of thirty roles, including Aida, Sieglinde, Elsa, and Madama Butterfly. This recipe was given by her husband, George Cehanovsky (1892–1986), also a Met singer for forty seasons, to Alfred Hubay, who was the Box Office Manager of the Met for many years.

Suprême of Chicken Rossini

2 large chicken breasts, boned, skinned, and cut
  in half
Salt and pepper to taste
⅓ cup flour
¼ cup (½ stick) butter
4 slices pâté de foie gras, about ¼ inch thick
2 black truffles, sliced
¼ cups dry sherry

Flatten the chicken breasts slightly, season with salt and pepper, and dredge lightly in flour. In a skillet, heat butter and sauté chicken for 3 minutes. Turn and sauté on the other side for 2 more minutes. Transfer chicken to a warm serving dish.

Sauté pâté slices for a minute in the butter remaining in the skillet. Place on top of chicken, then top with sliced truffles. Over high heat deglaze skillet with sherry, then spoon over chicken and serve. *Serves 4.*

Lawrence Tibbett
Chicken Casserole

¼ cup (½ stick) butter
1 chicken (about 3 pounds), cut up
¼ pound fresh mushrooms, sliced
3 celery hearts, sliced
1 medium onion, sliced
½ green bell pepper, seeded and sliced
1 cup tomato juice
Salt and pepper to taste
⅓ cup sour cream
1 cup cooked green peas
3 medium carrots, peeled, sliced, and cooked
*   until tender-crisp*
1 cup string beans, cooked until tender-crisp
½ cup dry white wine
1 tablespoon Worcestershire sauce

In a skillet, heat 2 tablespoons of the butter and brown the chicken on all sides over low heat. Remove chicken and keep warm. In a saucepan, heat remaining butter and add mushrooms, celery, onion, green pepper, and tomato juice. Season with salt and pepper. Mix well, cover, and simmer for 45 minutes. A few minutes before the sauce has finished cooking, stir in sour cream.

Preheat oven to 325 degrees. Put the sauce in the bottom of a large casserole, add the chicken pieces, and fill in spaces with the cooked vegetables. Add the wine and Worcestershire sauce, cover, and bake for about 15 minutes. *Serves 4.*

Lawrence Tibbett (1896–1960) first sang at the Met in 1923, and gave the company twenty-seven seasons in leading baritone roles. He was especially known for his Rigoletto, Germont in La Traviata, Scarpia in Tosca, and Amonasro in Aida. He also appeared in several Hollywood films.

From a 1933 Met program.

Mrs. Ezra K. Zilkha
Chicken in Pomegranate–Walnut Sauce

6 tablespoons (¾ stick) butter
1 medium onion, finely chopped
¼ teaspoon turmeric
¼ teaspoon black pepper
3 pounds chicken breast meat, cut into small
  pieces
Salt
Flour for dredging
2 cups coarsely chopped walnuts
2 cups fresh or canned pomegranate juice
1 cup fresh orange juice
1 cup hot water
1 tablespoon sugar

In a saucepan, heat 2 tablespoons of the butter, add the onion, turmeric, and pepper, then stir and sauté over medium heat until onion is golden, about 3 minutes.

In a skillet, heat remaining butter. Season the chicken pieces with salt and pepper, dredge in flour, and sauté until browned on both sides. Remove chicken from skillet and reserve.

Add walnuts to sautéed onions, stir, and sauté over low heat for 2 minutes; be careful—walnuts scorch easily. Add pomegranate and orange juices, hot water, and sugar, then season to taste with salt. Bring to a boil, add the chicken pieces, and simmer over low heat for about 30 minutes. There should be enough sauce to cover the chicken; if needed, add some hot water to keep chicken moist. Serve with rice or noodles. *Serves 6.*

Mrs. Ezra K. Zilkha
is a member of the Board of Directors
of the Metropolitan Opera Guild,
and a Managing Director of the
Metropolitan Opera Association.

Erin Langston
Mother's Curried Chicken

¼ cup (½ stick) butter
2 cups chopped onions
2½ cups peeled and chopped apples
2 cloves garlic, minced
4 cups chicken broth
1 tablespoon sugar
Salt and pepper to taste
1 cup flour mixed with 1½ cups broth or water
6 teaspoons curry powder, or to taste
⅓ cup lemon juice
4 cups chopped cooked chicken
Cooked white rice
Condiments: crumbled fried bacon, peanuts,
  sliced bananas, coconut, raisins, chopped hard-
  boiled eggs, and chutney

In a saucepan, heat butter and add onions, apples, and garlic. Mix and sauté for 3 or 4 minutes while stirring a few times. Add broth and sugar, season with salt and pepper, and bring to a simmer. While stirring with a spatula or wooden spoon, add mixed flour and broth until smooth and thickened. Add curry powder, lemon juice, and chicken. Mix well and simmer for 10 minutes. Serve over rice with the curry condiments. *Serves 4.*

Erin Langston
is secretary to the Managing Director and Board of Directors of the Metropolitan Opera Guild.

Shirley Bakal
Cassoulet Bakal

Sauce Base
1 medium onion, chopped
2 tablespoons (¼ stick) butter
Salt and pepper to taste
1 teaspoon dried basil
¼ cup dry white wine

Filling
1 whole chicken breast, boned and trimmed
1 pepperoni or hot Hungarian sausage, sliced
½ pound smoked ham, cut in strips
1 (12-ounce) can small white beans, drained

2 duck sausages (or ½ smoked duck), boned and sliced
½ cup dry white bread crumbs
1 teaspoon dried basil
Salt and pepper to taste
¼ cup dry white wine
3 tablespoons olive oil

Prepare sauce base first. Sauté onion in butter until translucent and soft, about 5 minutes. Season with salt and pepper, then add basil and white wine. Simmer for a minute or two.

Preheat oven to 375 degrees. Cover the bottom of a large casserole with one-third of the sauce base. Then make alternate layers with slices of chicken breast, sausage, ham strips, and beans. Follow with a layer of duck sausage or smoked duck and top with the remaining white beans. Cover with the remaining sauce base, sprinkle generously with bread crumbs, add basil, and season with salt and pepper. Combine wine and oil and sprinkle over the top. Bake until bubbly and well browned, about 25 minutes. *Serves 6.*

Shirley Bakal
is the Assistant to the Managing Director of the Metropolitan Opera Guild, and runs the Guild's Travel Program.

Yveta Synek Graff
Křepelky Pečené
ROAST QUAIL

4 quail
Salt to taste
2 ounces bacon, sliced
½ small onion, chopped (¼ cup)
¼ cup (½ stick) butter
1 cup water
3 black peppercorns
3 juniper berries, crushed
Lingonberries
Czech Dumplings (p. 169)

Preheat oven to 375 degrees. Wipe quail with a damp cloth, pat dry, and sprinkle with salt. Wrap the birds in bacon slices and secure with string. In a heatproof baking pan, sauté the onion in butter until soft, about 3 minutes. Add the quail and brown on both sides. Add ½ cup water, peppercorns, and juniper berries. Roast until birds are done, about 35 to 45 minutes. Baste frequently.

When quail are done, remove birds from pan. Skim fat from the pan juices, add the remaining ½ cup of water, bring to a boil, and deglaze the pan. Strain gravy, then serve birds with pan gravy, lingonberries, and dumplings. *Serves 2.*

Yveta Synek Graff has written about Czech opera for Opera News, *and has translated many of the works of Janáček, including* Jenůfa *for the Met's most recent revival. She is married to F. Malcolm Graff, Jr., who is the Secretary of the Metropolitan Opera Guild, and a Member of the Metropolitan Opera Association.*

Fedora Barbieri.
OPPOSITE: *Teresa Zylis-Gara.*

Sándor Kónya
Alföldi Paprikás Pulyka
PAPRIKA TURKEY FROM
THE HUNGARIAN PUSZTA

3 tablespoons lard

2 large onions, minced

1 tablespoon Hungarian sweet paprika

½ tablespoon Hungarian hot paprika or cayenne
   pepper to taste

3½ pounds raw boneless turkey meat (dark and
   white), cubed

2 peeled tomatoes, fresh or canned

1 teaspoon salt, or to taste

1 cup sour cream

In a heavy saucepan, heat lard and sauté onions until they just start to color, about 3 minutes. Remove pan from heat, then stir in paprikas and turkey. Add tomatoes and season with salt. Cover tightly and cook slowly until meat is tender, about 1 hour.

When ready to serve, top each portion with sour cream. Serve with spaetzle, fresh boiled noodles or rice, and a Hungarian cucumber salad on the side. *Serves 6 to 8.*

*Sándor Kónya
has sung leading tenor roles internationally since the 1950s, concentrating on the Wagner repertory. He now lives in Stuttgart. "Jó étvágyat (bon appétit) to everyone!"*

Yveta Synek Graff
Holoubata s Nádivkou
STUFFED ROAST SQUAB

Squab

3 squab

Salt to taste

¼ cup (½ stick) butter

¼ cup water

Lingonberries

Czech Dumplings (p. 169)

Stuffing

¼ cup (½ stick) butter

2 eggs, separated

Salt to taste

1¼ cups fresh white bread crumbs

½ cup milk

Dash of mace

1 tablespoon minced fresh parsley

Clean squab, remove giblets, and loosen skin from breasts. Chop livers and set aside for stuffing.

To prepare stuffing, cream the butter and blend thoroughly with egg yolks. Season with salt. Soak bread crumbs in milk, squeeze dry, and add to butter mixture along with chopped livers, mace, and parsley; mix well. Stiffly beat the egg whites, then fold into stuffing mixture.

Preheat oven to 325 degrees. Stuff the body and neck cavity of each squab, close openings with toothpicks, and lace with thread. Sprinkle birds with salt and rub skins with butter. Melt remaining butter in a large roasting pan and add water. Lay in the squab and roast for 1 to 1½ hours. Baste a few times with pan juices, adding a little more water to pan if needed to keep birds moist. When done, remove toothpicks and serve with pan gravy, lingonberries, and dumplings. *Serves 3.*

Company members dining on the Met tour train.

Yveta Synek Graff comments: "The forests of Bohemia, which were a great source of musical inspiration to our composers such as Smetana and Dvořák, have always been full of game: hare and deer, and particularly the wild birds such as quail, pheasant, and squab. Game dishes are an important part of Czech cooking—hearty peasant fare best enjoyed at home rather than in a restaurant. In the recipes for Czech dishes, you can read the history of a family, handed down through the generations. These come from mine."

Riso all'Aglio
Renato Capecchi

Armenian Pilaf
Gary Lakes

Potato Dumplings
Kurt Baum

Vegetables Zasu Pitts
Mrs. Kenyon Boocock

Czech Dumplings
Yveta Synek Graff

Cumberland Sauce
Jules Bond

Salad Lakmé
Jules Bond

Lentil and Carrot Puree
Mrs. Richard K. Moore

Custard Corn Pudding
John Alexander

Stuffed Zucchini
Roberta Peters

Caper Sauce
Mrs. Randolph H. Guthrie, Jr.

Red Cabbage Salad
Erica Merkling

Ezio Pinza. OVERLEAF: *Roberta Peters's Stuffed Zucchini, and the mask she wore in* Un Ballo in Maschera. *Miss Peters is shown as Oscar.*

SIDE DISHES AND CONDIMENTS

Renato Capecchi
Riso all'Aglio
RICE WITH GARLIC

2½ tablespoons butter
4 cloves garlic, chopped
2 cups Italian Arborio rice
3½ cups chicken broth, heated to boiling
Salt and pepper to taste
Grated Parmesan cheese

Preheat oven to 350 degrees. In a large, heatproof casserole, heat 2 tablespoons butter, add garlic, and sauté very gently until garlic just starts to color, about 3 minutes. Add rice, mix well to coat with butter, then add the hot chicken broth and season with salt and pepper. Cook while stirring until the mixture starts to thicken. Cover the casserole, place in oven, and bake for 20 minutes. Remove from oven, spread top with remaining butter, sprinkle with cheese, and serve at once. *Serves 6 to 8.*

*Renato Capecchi
has sung leading baritone roles at the
Met since 1951, taking time out to
sing at La Scala, Covent Garden,
and other important international
houses.*

Gary Lakes
Armenian Pilaf

⅔ cup long-grain white rice
3 tablespoons butter
2½ cups thin egg noodles
1 cup chicken broth
⅔ cup water
Salt and pepper to taste

Place the rice in a strainer and rinse thoroughly under cold running water until the water runs clear. In a heavy saucepan, heat butter over medium heat. Place the uncooked noodles in the pan. Sauté, stirring constantly, until noodles are golden brown, 5 minutes.

Add the washed and drained rice, broth, and water. Season with salt and pepper. Let come to a full boil, stir a few times with a fork, then reduce heat, cover, and cook over low heat until liquid is absorbed and the pilaf is cooked and fluffy, about 15 to 17 minutes. While cooking, stir once with a fork. *Serves 6.*

*Gary Lakes
made his Met debut in 1986 and has
sung several tenor roles there since
then, including Siegmund in the
Met's new recording of Die Walküre.
He and his wife reside in Pittsburgh.
"This is my mother-in-law's family recipe.
It's a favorite of mine."*

Kurt Baum
Potato Dumplings

4 medium mealy potatoes
1 thick slice white bread, crust removed
2 tablespoons (¼ stick) butter, plus 3 tablespoons
   butter, melted
Large pinch of mace
1 small egg, beaten
½ cup flour
1 tablespoon cornstarch
Salt and pepper to taste

Cook potatoes in boiling salted water until soft, about 20 minutes. Drain, peel, and rub through a sieve or mash until smooth; let cool. Dice bread and sauté in 2 tablespoons butter until golden, then drain on paper towels.

Combine mashed potatoes, mace, egg, flour, and cornstarch; season with salt and pepper. Mix well and shape into balls about 1½ inches in diameter. Press 2 cubes of fried bread into each dumpling, making sure that the cubes are completely covered with the potato dough.

In a large pot with boiling salted water, cook the dumplings uncovered for 12 to 15 minutes, turning them occasionally. Do not crowd the dumplings; cook 2 separate batches if necessary. When cooked, drain well and serve with hot melted butter or gravy. *Makes about 18 dumplings.*

*Kurt Baum
was born in Prague, and sang leading tenor roles at the Met from 1941 until
1967. He lives in New York City.*

Mrs. Kenyon Boocock
Vegetables Zasu Pitts

¼ cup (½ stick) butter
4 to 5 shallots, minced
2 teaspoons minced fresh tarragon, or ½ teaspoon
   dried
1 teaspoon minced fresh chervil, or 1 tablespoon
   minced fresh parsley
3 green celery stalks, trimmed and chopped
½ pound fresh mushrooms (including stems),
   chopped
1 pound small zucchini, finely diced
Salt and pepper to taste

In a saucepan, heat butter and sauté shallots until soft, about 2 minutes; do not let brown. Add herbs and celery, then sauté until just tender (*al dente*), about 5 minutes. Add mushrooms and zucchini, and cook until just tender, about 3 minutes. Season with salt and pepper. *Serves 4.*

*Mrs. Kenyon Boocock
is on the Emeritus Council of the
Metropolitan Opera Guild, and is an
Honorary Director of the Metropolitan
Opera Association. This recipe was given
to her by her friend the late Zasu Pitts.*

Yveta Synek Graff
Czech Dumplings

HOUSKOVÝ KNEDLÍK

4 cups sifted flour
1 teaspoon salt
2 egg yolks
1½ cups milk
4 cups diced stale white bread

Place flour in a mixing bowl. In another bowl lightly beat the salt, egg yolks, and milk. Pour into the flour and work dough until it is shiny and pulls away from the bowl. Cover and let stand for 1 hour.

Work diced bread into the dough. With floured hands, shape the dough into 3 or 4 rolls 8 inches long and about 2½ inches across. In a large pan, bring 6 quarts of water to a boil, put in the rolls, making sure that they don't stick to the bottom. Cover pan and cook for about 20 minutes, turning rolls once during cooking.

Remove rolls from pan with a large skimmer (or with 2 plates). Make a cut across the center of 1 roll to make sure it is cooked through. (Dough will not be gummy.) If not done, return to pot and cook 2 to 3 minutes more. Slice rolls with a sharp knife or with a piece of thread into ¾-inch-thick rounds. Arrange rounds in a heated bowl and serve with game, roast meats, or stews. *Serves 6 to 8.*

Note Leftover slices are excellent, quickly sautéed and browned in butter.

Jules Bond
Cumberland Sauce

2 tablespoons sliced orange peel, in fine julienne
   strips
1 tablespoon sliced lemon peel, in fine julienne
   strips
1½ cups red currant jelly
¼ cup Port wine
5 tablespoons orange juice
1 tablespoon lemon juice
½ teaspoon dry mustard
Pinch of ground ginger

Simmer orange and lemon peels in boiling water for 5 minutes; drain well. In the top of a double boiler, melt currant jelly over simmering water. Add all other ingredients, including drained peels, and blend well. Chill for several hours before serving. Serve with game, cold roast meats, or the Ham Mousse on page 32. *Makes about 1½ cups.*

OPPOSITE: *Edita Gruberova slicing Czech dumplings.*

Jules Bond
Salad Lakmé

Salad

1 small head cauliflower
12 small cherry tomatoes
1 bunch watercress

Herb Vinaigrette

¼ cup white wine vinegar
½ teaspoon dry mustard
2 teaspoons minced fresh parsley
2 teaspoons minced fresh chives
1 teaspoon minced fresh tarragon, or pinch of
    dried
1 teaspoon minced fresh chervil, or pinch of dried
2 teaspoons grated shallots
Salt and pepper to taste
½ cup vegetable oil

Prepare the dressing first. Blend vinegar and mustard, add herbs and shallots, and season with salt and pepper. Blend well, then add oil and blend again. Set aside.

Separate cauliflower into small florets, then cook in lightly salted boiling water until barely tender, about 3 or 4 minutes. Drain and cool. Heap the cauliflower in a salad bowl, and surround with cherry tomatoes and small bunches of watercress. Spoon dressing over the salad. *Serves 6.*

*Salad Lakmé
is one of many recipes named after operas. As the popular entertainment of the nineteenth and early twentieth centuries, operas often lent their names to dishes; in addition to this recipe, there were Soupe Tosca, Eggs Rienzi, Eggs Lakmé, Eggs Manon, Sole Traviata, Quails Carmen, and Salads Aida, Manon, and Mignon.*

Mrs. Richard K. Moore
Lentil and Carrot Puree

1½ cups lentils
2 tablespoons minced onion
1 teaspoon minced garlic
6 tablespoons (¾ stick) butter
2 teaspoons lemon juice
Salt and pepper to taste
8 large carrots, peeled
2 tablespoons sugar (brown or granulated)
¾ cup half heavy cream and half milk, scalded
2 tablespoons minced scallions
2 tablespoons minced parsley

Pick over and rinse lentils, then soak in cold water for about 1 hour. Drain, place in a saucepan, and add enough water to cover lentils by about 2 inches. Add onion and garlic, then cook over medium heat until just soft, about 45 minutes. Do not overcook. Drain well.

In a skillet, heat 2 tablespoons butter, add the drained lentils and lemon juice, then season with salt and pepper. Toss lightly until well combined. Place mixture in a bowl of a food processor, and process *lightly* for a few seconds. The texture should be fairly coarse and nutty.

Preheat oven to 225 degrees. Put carrots in a saucepan, add 1 tablespoon sugar and a pinch of salt, cover with water, and boil until carrots are tender, about 5 minutes. Drain and mash carrots with 2 tablespoons butter, add remaining sugar, and season with salt and pepper to taste. While whisking, add the cream—milk mixture and blend until smooth and fluffy. Combine lentils and carrots, put in a buttered large baking dish, sprinkle with minced scallions and parsley, and dot with bits of remaining butter. *Serves 4 to 6.*

Mrs. Richard K. Moore is a member of the Board of Directors of the Metropolitan Opera Guild, an Advisory Director to the Metropolitan Opera Association, and is on the Council of the Friends of Covent Garden. She divides her time between London and New York City.

John Alexander
Custard Corn Pudding

2 eggs
1½ teaspoons salt
1 teaspoon sugar
¼ teaspoon black pepper
12 ounces fresh-cut corn kernels, or 1 (12-ounce) can corn, drained
2 cups milk
2 tablespoons (¼ stick) butter, melted and hot

Preheat oven to 325 degrees. Butter a 1½-quart casserole. In a bowl, beat eggs, salt, sugar, and pepper with a wire whisk until smooth. Stir in corn and blend well. While whisking constantly, gradually add milk and butter. Pour mixture into casserole. Set casserole in a shallow pan, and fill pan with hot water coming half way up the side of the casserole. Bake until a knife inserted in the center comes out clean, about 1 hour. *Serves 6.*

John Alexander has sung leading tenor roles at the Met for over twenty-five years. He and his wife now live in Cincinnati. "This is one of my favorite recipes, handed down in my family from Mississippi."

Roberta Peters
Stuffed Zucchini

4 zucchini (about 2 pounds)
2 tablespoons (¼ stick) butter
2 scallions, chopped
½ pound fresh mushrooms, chopped
½ cup chopped walnuts
1 cup fresh bread crumbs
4 eggs
2 tablespoons chopped fresh parsley
1 tablespoon chopped fresh basil
Salt and pepper to taste
½ cup grated Parmesan cheese

Roberta Peters in her kitchen, c. 1950.

Preheat oven to 350 degrees. Butter a large baking dish. Scrub zucchini, cut in half lengthwise, and scoop out centers, leaving shells about ¼ inch thick. Reserve the pulp. Parboil the shells in lightly salted water for a minute or two, then drain well.

Chop the zucchini pulp and sauté in butter for a few minutes. Add the scallions and mushrooms, and sauté for 3 to 4 minutes. Mix in walnuts and remove from heat. Add bread crumbs. Beat eggs with the herbs, salt, and pepper, then add to pan. Mix well and use to fill the zucchini shells. Top with grated cheese.

Place zucchini in baking dish, put the dish in a larger pan, and add ½ inch of hot water to the pan. Bake until lightly brown on top, about 25 minutes. *Serves 4.*

Roberta Peters
was just twenty years old when she
made her Met debut in 1950, and
since then has sung thirty-five sea-
sons with the company. Best known
for her coluratura roles, she has
appeared at opera houses as diverse
as Salzburg and the Bolshoi, as well
as frequently in recital and on tele-
vision. Miss Peters has recorded most
of her best-known roles.

Mrs. Randolph H. Guthrie, Jr.
Caper Sauce

¼ cup Dijon mustard
2 cloves garlic, pressed
2 scant tablespoons white wine vinegar
Freshly ground black pepper to taste
4–5 tablespoons dry white wine
2 (3½-ounce) jars small capers, drained, with
    liquid reserved from 1 jar
1 teaspoon dark brown sugar
½ cup virgin olive oil

Whisk ingredients together, including the liquid from 1 jar of capers. Puree half the mixture in a blender, then combine it with the other half. Serve with fish or roasted meats. *Makes about 1 cup.*

Mrs. Randolph H. Guthrie, Jr. is a member of the Board of Directors of the Metropolitan Opera Guild and a Managing Director of the Metropolitan Opera Association. She has added: "This sauce is excellent with broiled fish, such as swordfish. Serve at room temperature. For roasts such as lamb, heat the sauce gently but do not let boil. The sauce will keep for weeks if refrigerated. I generally have a jar on hand to dress up a simple meal for last-minute guests."

Erica Merkling
Red Cabbage Salad

1 tablespoon vegetable oil
1 tablespoon caraway seed
1 tablespoon coriander seed
1 medium onion, thinly sliced
1 medium head red cabbage, cored and thinly
    sliced
1 apple, peeled and grated
1 cup orange or apple juice
⅓ cup mild vinegar, such as Japanese rice vinegar
2 tablespoons sugar, or more to taste
1 teaspoon grainy mustard
Salt to taste
Sour salt (see Note)

In a deep saucepan or Dutch oven, heat oil and add caraway, coriander, and onion. Sauté until onion is transparent and soft, about 3 minutes; do not brown. Add red cabbage, grated apple, and remaining ingredients. Mix well, cover tightly, and cook over medium heat until cabbage is wilted but still crisp, about 8 minutes. Correct seasoning; if a tangier taste is wanted, add more sour salt. *Serves 6.*

Note Sour salt is crystallized citric acid, available on the spice shelves of most markets.

Crème Brûlée
Mrs. Alexander M. Laughlin

Crema al Mascarpone
Maria Callas

Mousse au Chocolat
Martial Singher

Delicious Rice Pudding
James H. Naples

Great Aunt Kate's Steamed Blueberry Pudding
Mary Curtis-Verna

Trifle for a "Do"
Kent Cottam

Oranges Romeo and Juliet alla Veronese
Dario Soria

Plum or Apricot Dumplings
Jarmila Novotná

Strawberries Romanoff
Mrs. Charles Gilman, Sr.

Plättar
Kerstin Thorborg

Coupe Patti

Peach Melba

Blintzes Soufflé
Lisa Goldstein

Hot Molasses Soufflé with Cold Sauce
Gladys Swarthout

Orange Pudding
Diana Montague

Anooshabour
Lucine Amara

Apple Crunch
Leontyne Price

My Grandmother's Treacle Pudding
Mrs. Richard K. Moore

Kugel
Sara Tucker

Lemon Mousse
G. Palmer LeRoy

Vanilla Sauce
Jules Bond

OPPOSITE: *Frieda Hempel.* OVERLEAF: *Lucine Amara's Anooshabour, with the scarf she used in* Madama Butterfly, *and her headband from* Aida. *Miss Amara is shown as Rosalinda.*

DESSERTS

Mrs. Alexander M. Laughlin
Crème Brûlée

1 quart heavy cream
¼ cup sugar
1 tablespoon vanilla extract
Pinch of salt
8 egg yolks
Brown sugar

Preheat oven to 350 degrees. In a heavy saucepan, combine cream, sugar, vanilla, and salt. Heat very slowly until cream is scalded, stirring often; do not let come to boil. Beat egg yolks in a bowl until lemon colored. While stirring, very slowly add the scalded cream and stir until smooth and well mixed. Pour the custard into a 2-quart casserole and place it in a large baking dish. Pour in enough hot water to come half way up the casserole. Bake until a knife inserted in the custard comes out clean, about 25 to 30 minutes. Remove casserole from pan, cool, then refrigerate overnight.

Preheat the broiler. Sift brown sugar evenly, about ¼ inch thick, over the very cold custard. Place the casserole 6 to 8 inches from the broiler, turn the casserole a few times for even broiling, and watch carefully to prevent sugar from burning. Broil until sugar has melted and browned, about 1 to 2 minutes. Remove from oven, cool, and refrigerate for about 2 hours. Serve cold. The caramel will stay hard for 4 to 6 hours; do not store too long. *Serves 6 to 8.*

Mrs. Alexander M. Laughlin
is a member of the Board of Directors
of the Metropolitan Opera Guild
and a Managing Director of the
Metropolitan Opera Association.

Maria Callas
Crema al Mascarpone

3 eggs, separated
3 heaping tablespoons sugar
10 ounces mascarpone cheese
Cordial or other liqueur for flavoring to taste

Beat the egg whites until stiff. Combine egg yolks and sugar and beat until light and creamy. Add mascarpone to the beaten egg yolks, stir gently until well blended, then fold in the beaten egg whites. Gently stir in the liqueur of your choice to flavor the mixture. Serve in dessert dishes and garnish as desired. *Serves 4 to 6.*

Elisabeth Schwarzkopf, L.J. Brown of EMI Records, and Maria Callas.

Maria Callas (1923–1977) probably the most famous soprano of this century, sang only twenty times at the Met, and created controversy with her performances both on and off stage. On the same page as one of her recipes she wrote of her preferred postperformance meal: "After performances I love a hot light broth with some lemon squeezed in, some red meat cooked plain, like roast beef or hamburger or filet—very rare all of them—and salad."

Martial Singher
Mousse au Chocolat

2 ounces semisweet chocolate
2 tablespoons water
1 teaspoon very strong black coffee
1 tablespoon butter
1 egg, separated
Pinch of salt

In the top of a double boiler, melt chocolate over simmering water. Add water and coffee, and stir until smooth. Add the butter and egg yolk, stir and blend well, then simmer for another minute. Remove from heat and let cool.

Beat the egg white with the salt until stiff. Fold into the chocolate mixture. Place in a serving dish and chill for several hours or overnight. Serve and enjoy. *Serves 1.*

Martial Singher was a preeminent French baritone at the Met during the 1940s and '50s, singing Verdi and light Wagner roles as well. Since his retirement he has lived and taught singing in Santa Barbara, California. Of his recipe he notes, "There is no dessert I like better than a genuine French Mousse au Chocolate, and nobody makes a more delicious and light one than a friend of mine in my hometown of Biarritz. She was kind enough to give us her recipe when we last saw her and were treated to her mousse."

James H. Naples
Delicious Rice Pudding

1 navel orange
1 quart milk
½ cup sugar
¾ teaspoon salt
½ cup long-grain white rice
1 cup heavy cream, plus additional for whipping
2 egg yolks, lightly beaten
½ teaspoon vanilla extract
Cinnamon sugar (1 part sugar, 1 part ground cinnamon)

Peel orange like an apple, going round and round to remove peel in a long spiral. Scald milk in top of double boiler over boiling water. Add orange peel, sugar, salt, and rice and stir and mix well. Cover and cook until rice is tender, about 45 minutes. Stir a few times with a fork during the first part of the cooking. When rice is tender, remove and discard orange peel.

In a bowl, blend cream and beaten egg yolks. Add a few tablespoons of hot rice, blend well, then stir yolk mixture into the rice. Continue cooking in double boiler over simmering water until the pudding thickens, about 20 minutes, stirring a few times. Add vanilla, and remove from heat.

Spoon into dessert dishes and let cool or chill, if desired. Sprinkle with cinnamon sugar and garnish with whipped cream. *Serves 8.*

James H. Naples is the House Manager of the Metropolitan Opera. This recipe is from his wife, Nancy, who notes that "even if you are not a rice-pudding fan, this will convert you."

Mary Curtis-Verna
Great Aunt Kate's Steamed Blueberry Pudding

Pudding
½ cup (1 stick) butter
½ cup sugar
2 cups flour
Small pinch of salt
1 teaspoon baking soda
⅔ cup milk
1 teaspoon distilled white vinegar
1 tablespoon molasses
1 egg, lightly beaten
2 cups small fresh blueberries

Peach or Raspberry Sauce
½ cup (1 stick) butter, softened
1 cup confectioner's sugar
1 ripe peach, peeled and mashed, or ½ cup mashed raspberries

Lightly grease a 2-quart pudding mold or bowl. Cream butter and sugar until light. Mix in flour, salt, and baking soda. While stirring, add milk and vinegar and work until smooth. Mix in molasses and the egg. When blended, fold in the blueberries.

Pour batter into pudding mold or bowl, cover, and place on a rack in a pan with water coming two-thirds up the side of the mold. Cover and steam for 2½ hours. Add more boiling water, if needed, to keep up water level.

While pudding steams, prepare sauce. Cream butter and confectioner's sugar. When light, add the peach or raspberries and stir well. Serve with hot pudding. *Serves 6 to 8.*

Mary Curtis-Verna sang leading soprano roles at the Met for ten seasons, beginning in 1957. She now teaches singing at the University of Washington in Seattle, and notes that "this recipe has been in the family for a hundred years."

Kent Cottam
Trifle for a "Do"

Cake

1 cup sifted flour
4 eggs, room temperature
½ cup sugar
1 teaspoon vanilla extract
¼ teaspoon salt

Crème Anglaise

1½ cups milk
4 egg yolks
1 cup sugar
1 teaspoon cornstarch
2 tablespoon white Port wine

Fruits and Flavoring

½ cup white Port wine
¾ cup apricot jam
4 ripe peaches, sliced and lightly sugared
1 pint strawberries, hulled and halved, then
    lightly sugared
1 cup heavy cream, whipped with 1½
    tablespoons sugar and 1 tablespoon Framboise
    brandy

First prepare the cake. Preheat oven to 400 degrees. Butter an 8-inch square straight-sided cake pan. Dust with 2 tablespoons flour and tap out excess. Cut a wax paper liner to fit the bottom of the pan and insert it.

In a large bowl, mix eggs and sugar, set over just-simmering water, and stir constantly until the eggs warm; do not let the water boil. Remove from heat, add vanilla, and beat with an electric mixer until the mixture is about 3 times its original volume, almost white and quite thick. Mix remaining flour and the salt, sprinkle one-third of the flour over the egg mixture, and with a rubber spatula gently fold the flour into the eggs. Repeat with the next third and then with the remaining flour. Pour the mixture into the baking pan, smooth the top, and bake in the center of the oven for 20 to 25 minutes.

Remove cake from oven and cool on a rack for 10 minutes. Run a knife around the sides of the pan, invert onto a rack, remove pan, and peel off wax paper. Leave the cake to cool completely. It is even better when slightly stale.

Scald milk for the crème. In the top of a double boiler, combine egg yolks, sugar, and cornstarch. Whip until creamy and pale and mixture ribbons from beater. Place over simmering water, then whisk in hot milk and wine. Stir constantly until the back of a spoon is coated. Immediately put pan into cold water for 10 seconds, then replace over hot water and remove the double boiler from the stove.

Slice the cake horizontally in half. Into a large glass serving bowl, place 1 layer of cake. Sprinkle with half the Port wine. Spread with apricot jam. Arrange sliced peaches on top. Add half the crème Anglaise and spread it evenly. Add the second cake layer, sprinkle with remaining Port, and spread with jam. Arrange berries over this layer, add the remaining crème Anglaise, spread evenly, and mound the whipped cream on top. *Serves 4 to 6.*

*Kent Cottam
is a tenor in the Metropolitan Opera
Chorus.*

Dario Soria
Oranges Romeo and Juliet alla Veronese

6 navel oranges
1¼ cups sugar

Peel the oranges and cut the peels into thin julienne strips. Cut all the white pith off the peels. Place water in a deep saucepan and bring to a boil; add ¼ cup sugar, put the peeled oranges in the pan and boil until the oranges float to the surface. Remove immediately, cool, and refrigerate.

To 4 cups of the water in which the oranges were boiled, add remaining

From a Met program, 1932.

sugar and bring to a boil again. Add the julienned orange peels and boil gently until the peels are candied, about 1 to 1¼ hours. Remove from heat and cool. To serve, put candied strips on the whole chilled oranges and spoon the remaining syrup over them. Serve with fruit knife and fork. *Serves 6.*

*Dario Soria (1912–1980)
founded both Cetra-Soria and Angel
Records and produced the deluxe
Soria Series of records for RCA, as
well as the Metropolitan Opera
Historic Broadcast recordings. He
was Managing Director of the Guild
from 1970 until 1977. This recipe
appears through the kindness of
Mrs. Soria.*

Jarmila Novotná
Plum or Apricot Dumplings

4 cups flour
2 eggs, lightly beaten
Light cream or milk
Pinch of salt
1 pound Italian prune plums or small apricots
Sugar dots (small cubes)
Fried soft bread crumbs, sieved farmer cheese, or
    ground poppy seeds, for garnish
Melted butter
Confectioner's sugar

Mix flour and beaten eggs, then add enough cream or milk to make a stiff dough. Add salt, beat and knead well, then roll out the dough to about ½ inch thick. Cut the dough into 3-inch squares.

Remove pits from plums or apricots but do not cut the fruit in half. Place a sugar dot into each fruit, then shape the squares of dough around each plum or apricot to encase it completely, pinching the edges together to prevent water from seeping into the dumpling.

Place the dumplings, not too many at a time, into boiling lightly salted water and boil for about 10 minutes. Drain well, arrange dumplings on a heated platter, sprinkle with bread crumbs, farmer cheese, or poppy seeds, then spoon a little melted butter over them. When served, the dumplings are torn in half with 2 forks and liberally sprinkled with sugar. *Serves about 6.*

Mrs. Charles Gilman, Sr.
Strawberries Romanoff

1 quart strawberries
¼ cup sugar, or to taste
2 ounces (¼ cup) brandy
2 ounces (¼ cup) Curaçao liqueur
1 cup whipped cream
1½ quarts vanilla ice cream, slightly softened

Hull strawberries. Add sugar, brandy, and liqueur, then mix gently and let stand for 30 minutes. Mix whipped cream and ice cream (the mixture should be on the soft side), spoon over berries, and serve. *Serves 6 to 8.*

Note Raspberries or pitted black cherries can replace the strawberries.

*Mrs. Charles Gilman, Sr.
is a member of the Board of Directors
of the Metropolitan Opera Guild
and a Member of the Metropolitan
Opera Association.*

Carole Malone as Gretel and Paul Franke as the Witch in Hansel and Gretel.

Kerstin Thorborg
Plätter

SWEDISH PANCAKES

3 eggs
1 cup heavy cream
1 heaping cup flour
2½ cups milk
½ teaspoon salt
3½ tablespoons butter, melted
Strawberry jam or lingonberry preserves

Whisk the eggs, add cream, and then whisk in flour. Add milk gradually, along with salt and 1½ tablespoons melted butter. Stir well, then rest batter for 2 hours.

Heat a pancake griddle, and brush with some remaining melted butter. Stir the batter well and drop onto griddle to make small (3 to 5-inch) thin and light pancakes. Cook until lightly browned on both sides, about 1 to 2 minutes each side. Serve with jam or preserves. *Serves 4.*

Note The pancakes can also be made with only milk.

Kerstin Thorborg (1896–1970) was one of the Met's most beloved mezzo-sopranos. After her debut in 1936, she sang 243 performances of nineteen roles, including many with Flagstad and Melchior. She wrote of this recipe, "These pancakes are usually served as dessert. In almost every Swedish home, even at the King's table, this dish is served with every Thursday dinner."

Coupe Patti

½ cup sugar
1 cup water
3 white peaches, peeled and sliced
6 fresh apricots, pitted and cut in half
1 cup fresh pineapple cubes
1 pint fresh raspberries
1½ cups Champagne

In a saucepan, simmer sugar and water for 5 minutes. Remove from heat, cool, and then chill. Chill the fruit.

In a serving bowl, place the well-chilled fruit and add the chilled syrup. Mix gently, then pour the Champagne into the bowl. Place bowl in a pan of crushed ice and let stand for 2 hours before serving. *Serves 6.*

Coupe Patti
was named after the celebrated soprano Adelina Patti (1843–1919).
Born in Madrid, Patti studied in
New York and made her debut at
sixteen at the Academy of Music,
New York's major opera theater
before the Met was founded. She
sang only a few times at the Met but
was one of the most famous performers of her time, the kind of celebrity
who inspired the great chefs of the
nineteenth century.

Peach Melba

White freestone peaches
Vanilla ice cream, slightly softened
Fresh raspberry puree, sweetened

Dip the peaches in boiling water for 1 minute, remove, and dip in ice water. Slip off skins, cut the peaches in half, and chill.

Put softened ice cream in a serving bowl or individual cups, arrange peach halves on top and cover with the sweetened raspberry puree. Serve at once.

Peach Melba
was created by Escoffier for Nellie Melba in 1905, for the opening of the Carlton Hotel in London. In the original recipe the peaches are just dipped in boiling water and peeled. In most current recipes, the peach halves are poached for a few minutes in a light vanilla-flavored syrup.

Lisa Goldstein
Blintzes Soufflé

½ cup (1 stick) butter
12 frozen blintzes (6 cheese, 6 fruit)
1 pint sour cream
4 eggs
½ cup sugar
1 teaspoon vanilla extract
2 tablespoon orange juice

Preheat oven to 350 degrees. Melt butter. Place blintzes in a large, rectangular baking dish. In a blender, combine all other ingredients and the melted butter. Blend until frothy, then pour mixture over blintzes. Bake uncovered for 45 minutes. *Serves 6.*

Lisa Goldstein
is fourteen years old, and has been singing in the Met's Children's Chorus for four years.

OPPOSITE (BOTH): *Adelina Patti.* THIS PAGE (BOTH): *Nellie Melba.*

Gladys Swarthout with her husband, Frank Chapman.

Gladys Swarthout
Hot Molasses Soufflé with Cold Sauce

Soufflé

3 tablespoons butter
¼ cup flour
¾ cup milk
½ cup molasses
¼ teaspoon ground ginger
¼ teaspoon ground cinnamon
Pinch of salt
4 eggs, separated
2 tablespoons sugar

Cold Sauce

2 eggs
½ cup sugar
1 cup heavy cream, stiffly whipped
Rum or cognac to taste

For sauce, beat eggs and sugar until light. Add whipped cream and flavor with rum or cognac. Chill as cold as you can without actually freezing.

In saucepan, melt butter, add flour, and stir. Add milk gradually, stirring well. Add molasses, spices, and salt, and allow to cool.

Preheat oven to 375 degrees. Butter a 2-quart soufflé dish. Beat egg yolks and sugar until thick, then add to the mixture. Beat the egg whites until stiff, then fold into mixture. Pour into soufflé dish and bake for 50 minutes. Serve hot with chilled sauce. *Serves 8.*

Gladys Swarthout (1900–1969) was a leading mezzo-soprano at the Met for some thirteen seasons, singing 162 performances from 1929 until 1934. She also appeared in several films. She described this recipe as "a three-way collaboration between our cook, Mr. Chapman (her husband), and myself."

Renata Tebaldi as Tosca.

Diana Montague
Orange Pudding

½ cup (1 stick) butter

1 cup superfine sugar

1 cup self-rising flour, or 1 cup all-purpose flour
  mixed with 1 teaspoon baking powder

½ cup fresh white bread crumbs

2 eggs, lightly beaten

Pinch of salt

Grated zest of 2 oranges

Juice of 2 oranges

Vanilla Sauce (page 193)

Lightly grease a 1½-quart pudding mold or deep bowl. Cream butter with sugar until light and fluffy. Add all other ingredients and mix well. Pour into pudding mold, cover tightly with foil, and place in larger pot. Pour in enough hot water to come two-thirds up side of mold, then cover lightly and steam for 1½ hours. Serve with sauce. *Serves 4.*

Diana Montague
made her Met debut in 1987 as
Annio in Mozart's La Clemenza
di Tito. She lives in Hampshire,
England.

Lucine Amara
Anooshabour
ARMENIAN CHRISTMAS
PUDDING

1 cup hulled whole wheat berries, or medium
* pearled barley*
3 quarts water
1½ cups golden raisins
1½ cups dried apricots
1 cup blanched almonds, plus additional for
* garnish*
2 cups sugar
2 tablespoons rosewater (available in drugstores)
Walnut halves, for garnish

Rinse wheat berries under cold running water. Place in a large saucepan, add water, bring to a boil, then take off the heat. Cover and let soak overnight.

Next day, cook berries over low heat for 1½ hours. Rinse raisins and apricots, then cut apricots in quarters. Add both to the wheat, along with the almonds and sugar. Mix and cook for another 30 minutes. Take off the heat, mix in rosewater, then pour the mixture into a deep dish or serving bowl. Garnish top with additional almonds and walnuts. Chill before serving. *Serves about 20.*

Lucine Amara
made her Met debut on opening
night of Rudolf Bing's first season,
1950, and has since sung over 450
performances of more than forty roles
with the company. She is Armenian,
and notes that "this is one of my
favorite Christmas recipes."

Leontyne Price
Apple Crunch

1 (21-ounce) can apple pie filling
½ cup granulated sugar
1 teaspoon ground cinnamon
2 teaspoons lemon juice
¼ cup water
¾ cup quick-cooking oatmeal
¾ cup dark brown sugar
½ cup flour
1 teaspoon baking powder
½ cup (1 stick) butter, softened

Preheat oven to 375 degrees. Lightly grease a 9-inch pie plate. Mix filling, granulated sugar, cinnamon, lemon juice, and water. Place mixture in pie plate. Blend oatmeal, brown sugar, flour, and baking powder, then, with your hands, work in the butter and pat the mixture over the apples. Bake until

top is browned and crisp, about 45 minutes. *Serves 4 to 6.*

Mrs. Richard K. Moore
My Grandmother's Treacle Pudding

Equipment needed: a household scale and 2 [1½-quart] molds with tight-fitting cover, such as a plum pudding mold.

6 extra-large eggs
Sugar [about 1½ cups]
Butter [about 1½ cups, or 3 sticks], softened
Sifted flour [about 3 cups]
Each of the above 3 ingredients of the same weight as the eggs.

4 teaspoons baking powder
¾ cup milk
Heavy cream, whipped until thickened
Treacle or Lyle's Golden Syrup
Strawberries (optional)

Resift the measured flour with the baking powder and set aside. Beat the butter with the sugar and eggs until light and fluffy. Beat in the flour mixture, then add milk and beat again. Cover with cloth and let rest for 3 hours.

Lightly grease pudding molds or bowls, then coat insides with treacle. Beat batter again, then pour into molds, filling them not more than three-fourths full (the batter will rise). Cover each with a greased round of brown paper, close securely, and lower each mold into a large pot of boiling water and cover. The water level should be fairly high, but not high enough to seep into the mold. Make sure that molds are level and stand upright. Boil gently for about 3 hours, adding more water as needed to keep the water level the same.

Remove lids of molds to check if puddings are done; they should have risen and have many little air holes. Run a knife along the edge, give the mold a shake to loosen the pudding, and unmold each onto a serving platter. Best served warm, with the whipped cream. Dribble a bit of treacle on top of each serving, and add some berries, if desired. [*Each pudding serves 8 to 10.*]

Note Instead of making 2 puddings, half the batter can be used for cupcakes. Grease muffin tins and eliminate the treacle. Fill tins with batter and bake at 350 degrees until cupcakes spring back when touched in the center, about 25 minutes.

Sara Tucker
Kugel
NOODLE PUDDING

1 pound medium egg noodles

1½ cups sugar

6 eggs, separated

1 (16-ounce) can mixed fruit, drained

3 green apples, peeled, cored, and sliced

½ (8-ounce) jar maraschino cherries, drained and cut in half

1 teaspoon ground cinnamon

Pinch of grated nutmeg

½ cup (1 stick) butter, melted

Crumbled cornflakes

Preheat oven to 350 degrees. Lightly grease a 2-quart casserole or baking dish. Boil the noodles until done, and drain well. Blend sugar with lightly beaten egg yolks. Add mixed fruit, apples and cherries, cinnamon, and nutmeg. Mix well, then blend the mixture with the noodles. Beat egg whites until stiff, then fold in along with the melted butter. Put the mixture in casserole, then sprinkle cornflake crumbs on top. Bake for 1 hour. *Serves 6.*

Richard Tucker samples Sara's baking.

*Sara Tucker (1914–1985)
was the wife of the celebrated Met
tenor Richard Tucker (1913–1975).
She was a well-known figure in the
music world, and directed the
Richard Tucker Music Foundation,
which provides annual awards to
promising young singers and gives
grants to young-artists' programs.
This recipe appears through the
kindness of the Tucker family.*

G. Palmer LeRoy
Lemon Mousse

1 cup sugar
4 egg yolks
¼ cup lemon juice
1 package unflavored gelatin
¼ cup hot water
¼ cup cold water
6 egg whites, beaten until stiff

Blend sugar, egg yolks, and lemon juice and whisk until light colored. Dissolve gelatin in hot water, let stand for 5 minutes, then add the cold water. Fold egg whites and dissolved gelatin into the egg-yolk mixture, pour into a 1½-quart mold, and chill until well set, several hours (or overnight). *Serves 8.*

*G. Palmer LeRoy
is the Managing Director of the
Metropolitan Opera Guild. This is
a favorite family recipe, contributed
by his wife Kyra LeRoy.*

Jules Bond
Vanilla Sauce

1½ cups half and half or light cream
½ teaspoon vanilla extract
4 egg yolks
½ cup superfine sugar
1 tablespoon Grand Marnier or other orange
   liqueur

In the top of a double boiler, heat cream and vanilla extract over simmering water. In the meantime, place egg yolks, sugar, and liqueur in a bowl; whisk until light and fluffy. Add the heated cream, a little at a time, while whisking constantly until smooth. Return the mixture to the double boiler and stir until the sauce has thickened. Serve at once. *Makes about 1¾ cups.*

Lemon Sponge Cake
Mrs. Alexander Brand

Chocolate Roll with Cocoa Cream Filling
Kate Webb Harris

Quick Dessert Cake
Jessye Norman

Sponge Cake
Maria Callas

Brownie Pie
Arthur T. Stieren

Palmetto Cake
Lucinda W. Frame

Rocky's Bourbon Fruit Cake
Rockwell Blake

Raisin Cream-Cheese Pound Cake
Adrian Silva

Three Weeks' Cake
Theodor Uppman

Pecan-Rum Pie
Michael Devlin

Melitta's Ladyfinger Cake
Melitta Anderman

Ricotta Cheese Cake
Licia Albanese

Gâteau *La Dame Blanche*
Michel Sénéchal

Chocolate Mousse Pie
Ariel Bybee

Mother's Pumpkin Pie
Joyce Castle

Texas Pecan Pie
Timothy Jenkins

OPPOSITE: *The menu from the* Vanessa *premiere party, 1958. Both production and menu were designed by Cecil Beaton.* OVERLEAF: *Maria Callas's Sponge Cake, with a fan she used in* Madama Butterfly, *and Vincenzo Bellini's watch.*

CAKES AND PIES

Mrs. Alexander Brand
Lemon Sponge Cake

1 rounded cup sifted sugar
½ cup water
6 egg whites, stiffly beaten
6 egg yolks, beaten until quite thick
Juice of ½ lemon
1 rounded cup sifted cake flour

Preheat oven to 325 degrees. Lightly grease a 10-inch tube pan. In a saucepan, boil sugar and water until it spins threads (soft ball stage), 238 degrees on a candy thermometer. Add sugar syrup slowly to the beaten egg whites and beat until cool with a wire whisk. Whisk in beaten egg yolks and lemon juice. Fold in the flour, then pour mixture into cake pan and bake for 55 minutes. Invert pan and let cake cool before removing. *Serves about 6.*

Note This delicious, moist sponge cake takes only 20 minutes to prepare and mix.

*Mrs. Alexander Brand
is a member of the Board of Directors
of the Metropolitan Opera Guild.
She served for many years as Director of the Guild's Special Events and
Ticket Service Departments, and
organized the testing of recipes for
this book.*

Kate Webb Harris
Chocolate Roll with Cocoa Cream Filling

6 ounces semisweet chocolate
3 tablespoons cold strong coffee
6 eggs, separated
1 cup granulated sugar
Pinch of salt
1½ cups heavy cream
2 tablespoons unsweetened cocoa powder
½ teaspoon vanilla extract
Confectioner's sugar

Preheat oven to 350 degrees. Combine chocolate and coffee in the top of a double boiler, and put over simmering water until mixture is melted. Beat egg yolks until creamy, then gradually beat in ¾ cup sugar until the mixture is thick and light in color. Remove chocolate from heat and stir into the beaten egg yolks; blend well. Beat egg whites with salt until they form stiff but not dry peaks. Fold gently but thoroughly into the chocolate mixture.

Grease a 10 × 15-inch jelly-roll pan, line with wax paper, and grease the wax paper. With a spatula, spread the mixture evenly in the pan. Bake for 15 minutes. Place pan on a rack to cool, and cover top of the cake with a damp linen towel. After

about 1 hour, invert the cake onto towel. Remove the wax paper from the bottom of the cake.

Combine cream, remaining ¼ cup sugar, cocoa, and vanilla. Beat until stiff, but don't overbeat. Spread the mixture on the cooled cake and, lifting the towel on the bottom, roll up the cake lengthwise. Slide it, seam side down, onto a serving platter. Just before serving, sprinkle roll with sifted confectioner's sugar. *Serves 12 or more.*

*Kate Webb Harris
is a member of the Board of Directors
of the Metropolitan Opera Guild.*

Jessye Norman
Quick Dessert Cake

1¾ cups self-rising flour, or 1¾ cups all-purpose
    flour mixed with 2 teaspoons baking powder
¾ teaspoon salt
3 eggs, well beaten
¾ cup (1½ sticks) butter, softened
¾ cup dark brown sugar
¼ cup chopped blanched almonds
¼ cup raisins
1½ teaspoons lemon extract
¼ cup Grand Marnier or other orange-flavored
    liqueur
½ cup milk, approximately

In a large bowl, sift together flour and salt. Add all other ingredients except milk and beat with an electric mixer at medium speed for 4 minutes. While beating, add enough milk to make a fairly moist cake batter. Set batter aside for 10 minutes.

Preheat oven to 350 degrees. Grease and flour a 9-inch square cake pan. Beat batter again at high speed for 2 to 3 minutes. Pour batter into the pan and bake until cake springs back when pressed in center, about 45 to 50 minutes. Cool on a rack, then cut and serve. *Serves 8.*

*Jessye Norman
was born in Augusta, Georgia, and
sang leading roles in Europe for
fourteen years before making her
Met debut on opening night of the
Met's centennial season in 1983.
She has been back each year since
then, and has been seen on "Live
from the Met" in* Les Troyens,
Dialogues of the Carmelites, *and*
Ariadne auf Naxos. *She writes
that, "this cake makes a fine accompaniment to fresh fruit salads or ice
cream."*

Sponge cake – but not quite
(it) I like it better

4 eggs.
2 cups flour
2 teaspoons baking powder.
1 cup milk – hot.
any flavor – or lemon or
    raspery – banana – any kind.
½ teaspoon salt –
– Beat the egg whites –
with salt a cup of sugar – to
peaks – Then beat the yolks
with the flavoring & rest &
sugar. well. add slowly when eggs
yolks & sugar are light & fluffy
the hot milk. & then add the
flour a little at a time & mix
– delicately but thoroughly –
Then by hand add the
whites very delicately – &
immedeately put in tube pans
& in loaf pans – in preheated
oven 325 degrees for about ¾ to
one hour –
        Cool on rack away
from draft & turned upside
down so as it will not sit as
they say – decorate as you like

The flour should be sifted three times
with salt & baking powder

Maria Callas's recipe for Sponge Cake (see page 202).

Mr. and Mrs. Dario Soria
request the pleasure of your company
at a reception in honor of
Maria Meneghini Callas
following her Metropolitan Opera debut
on Monday Evening, October twenty-ninth

R. S. V. P.
38 West 48 Street   The Trianon Room
or Plaza 7-5910   Ambassador Hotel

Callas in the Kitchen

BY DORLE J. SORIA

Maria Callas—La Divina, diva, goddess, siren, tigress, mystery—all this is part of the standard Callas legend. Nobody thinks to recall that Callas was also a woman, a normal woman, and that she enjoyed doing all the things many women do. She loved to shop, to cook, to eat, and—like most women—she was on a diet.

When I first saw her in her own home it was in Verona, in 1954, shortly after her first famous *Tosca* Scala recording for Angel. She was living with her husband, Giovanni Battista Meneghini (whom she had met in Verona), in a penthouse of a palazzo, high over the city, overlooking the Arena where her first big success had been. Very much the proud young housewife, she showed us around the apartment and said she had two favorite rooms. The first was her music room with the piano where she practiced, the second was the kitchen. "I spend a lot of time there, cooking the special things we both love." When she came to New York we would go shopping together. Her first discovery was the five-and-ten where she plundered the shelves, buying every kind

of kitchen gadget. Then she found more elegant hardware and houseware stores, and when she went back to Italy her valises were bulging with pots and pans and cutlery, with whisks and blenders, and with fancy paper napkins and kitchen towels.

During her first season at the Chicago Lyric Opera, she and her husband had a suite with a kitchenette at the Ambassador Hotel. We found her there one day, busily boiling chicken. "Battista loves it, and I do too," she said. She would also make special dishes for him—pastas and polenta—but these she firmly denied herself. She compensated by cutting out recipes from glossy women's magazines and carefully saving them.

In our Angel Record days, we were planning a story about what Angel artists liked to eat, and we asked Maria for a favorite recipe and to tell us what she liked to eat after a performance. She was quite firm about her postopera meal—the usual broth, beef, salad—but her recipe revealed her secret craving. If you dined with Callas, for instance, she would always refuse dessert but then, when your own sweet arrived, she would always lean over and steal a bit. And so her recipe was for a dessert entitled "Sponge Cake,

But Not Quite It—I Like It Better." That was Maria Callas. She always found her own way better.

Dorle J. Soria
was married to Dario Soria, who
founded Angel Records. She worked
for many years as the company's
press director. She now serves as an
advisory director to the Met, and is
the co-producer of the Met's Historic
Broadcast series of recordings.

Maria Callas
Sponge Cake, But Not Quite It—I Like It Better

4 eggs, separated
1 cup sugar
2 cups flour
2 teaspoons baking powder
1 cup hot milk
1 teaspoon flavoring of your choice (lemon, raspberry, or other)
½ teaspoon salt

[Preheat oven to 325 degrees. Lightly grease a 9 × 5-inch loaf pan.]

Combine egg whites with ½ cup sugar and beat until they form peaks. In another bowl, beat egg yolks and remaining sugar until light and fluffy, then add slowly the hot milk while beating until well blended. Combine flour, baking powder, and salt; sift 3 times, then combine with the egg yolk mixture. Add flavoring, and mix gently but thoroughly. Fold in the beaten egg whites, pour mixture in loaf pan, [and] place the pan in another one filled with 1 inch of hot water. Bake at 325 degrees for about 45 minutes to an hour, until the cake tests done [until it springs back when pressed in center]. Cool on a rack [for 10 minutes] and turn it out immediately [and let cool completely]. It will not "sit," as they say. Decorate as you like.

[*Note* For greater volume when beating egg whites, beat the whites until they form soft peaks, then gradually add sugar and beat until they form stiff peaks—ed.]

Arthur T. Stieren
Brownie Pie

½ cup (1 stick) butter
1 ounce unsweetened chocolate
1 cup sugar
½ cup flour
2 eggs
1 teaspoon vanilla extract
¼ teaspoon salt
1 cup chopped pecans or walnuts

Dario Soria (left) with Maria Callas.

Preheat oven to 325 degrees. Lightly butter a 9-inch pie pan. In a saucepan, carefully melt the butter with the chocolate. Remove pan from heat and stir in the sugar, then the flour, then eggs, vanilla, and salt. Mix well, add the pecans, and pour mixture into pie pan. Bake for 25 to 30 minutes. Cool 10 minutes, then serve warm with coffee ice cream or whipped cream. *Serves 4 to 6.*

Arthur T. Stieren is a member of the Metropolitan Opera Association. This recipe was submitted by his wife, Jane, who adds that "the virtues of this recipe (I think) are many, simple and good being only two of them. It ranks high with me as an 'emergency dessert' and it never fails."

Lucinda W. Frame
Palmetto Cake

2 cups (1 pound) butter
2½ cups sugar
12 eggs
4½ cups sifted cake flour
1 teaspoon baking powder
¼ teaspoon salt
2 pounds shredded citron
1 pound grated coconut

Preheat oven to 325 degrees. Butter and lightly flour a 10-inch tube pan. Cream butter, add sugar, and beat until fluffy. Add eggs, 1 at a time, beating well after each addition. Sift flour with baking powder and salt, then gradually fold into egg mixture. Fold in citron and coconut. Pour batter into pan, and bake until center springs back when pressed in center, about 1½ hours. Let cool on a rack for 10 minutes, then remove cake from pan and let cool completely. *Serves 8 to 10.*

Note Sprinkle a little flour on the shredded citron to separate the pieces and keep them from sticking.

Lucinda W. Frame
is a member of the Board of Directors
of the Metropolitan Opera Guild.

Rockwell Blake
Rocky's Bourbon Fruit Cake

4 cups flour
1 teaspoon baking powder
1 teaspoon baking soda
2 cups dark brown sugar
1 cup water
1 cup vegetable shortening
2 teaspoons ground cinnamon
1 teaspoon ground cloves
1 teaspoon grated nutmeg
1 cup seedless raisins
1½ pounds mixed candied fruit
½ pound candied cherries
½ pound candied pineapple pieces
1 cup bourbon, plus ½ cup for pouring over (optional)
2 cups chopped pecans or walnuts

Sift together the flour, baking powder, and soda. Set aside. Combine brown sugar, water, shortening, spices, and fruits. Mix well, put into a large saucepan, and bring to a boil over high heat. Remove from heat, cover, and cool to room temperature.

Preheat oven to 300 degrees. Line a 10-inch round baking pan (the kind with a cover) with aluminum foil, leaving about 5 inches of excess foil all around the edge. (Foil will be folded over the top of the

On January 23, 1945, a gala was staged to celebrate the Metropolitan Opera Guild's tenth anniversary. Left to right, front row: the Guild's founder, Mrs. August Belmont, dancers from the Ballet, Lucrezia Bori, Frances Greer, Julia Barashkova, and Josef Carmassi. Back row: John Garris, James Melton, Marina Svetlova, Lily Djanel, Edward Johnson, Jarmila Novotná, Ella Fresch, and John Brownlee. In the cake was a gold purse containing a $30,000 donation from the Guild to the Met.

cake after it is baked and cooled.) Butter the foil.

Place fruit mixture in a bowl and add the dry mixture, bourbon, and nuts. Blend ingredients by hand. Pour into the pan and bake for 2½ hours.

Remove cake from oven and let stand, uncovered, until cool. When cool, you may spoon another ½ cup of bourbon over the cake. Fold over the foil to seal tightly and cover with lid. The cake im-

proves with age, though it can be eaten the day it was prepared. *Serves 12 to 16.*

Note For a nonalcoholic cake, substitute pineapple juice for the bourbon.

Rockwell Blake
won the first Richard Tucker award
in 1978. He first sang at the Met in
1981, and has returned for several
seasons since then.

Adrian Silva
Raisin Cream-Cheese Pound Cake

Cake

½ cup (1 stick) butter
8 ounces cream cheese
1¼ cups sugar
2 eggs
1 teaspoon vanilla extract
2 cups unsifted flour
½ teaspoon baking soda
½ teaspoon baking powder
¼ teaspoon salt
¼ cup milk
1 cup raisins

Topping

½ cup dark brown sugar
⅓ cup unsifted flour
½ teaspoon ground cinnamon
2 teaspoons (¼ stick) butter

Preheat oven to 325 degrees. Butter and flour a 9 × 13-inch baking pan.

Cream the butter and cream cheese until light, then gradually add the sugar and beat until fluffy. Beat in eggs (1 at a time) and vanilla until well blended. Set aside. Mix flour, baking soda, baking powder, and salt. Gradually add flour mixture to cheese mixture, alternating with milk and beating well after each addition. Add raisins and mix.

Pour batter into the baking pan. Mix the topping ingredients and sprinkle on the batter. Bake until a toothpick inserted in the center comes out clean, about 1 hour. Cool cake, then slice. *Serves 10 to 12.*

*Adrian Silva
is a customer representative for the
Marketing Department of the Met.*

Theodor Uppman
Three Weeks' Cake

2 cups water
2 cups sugar
1 pound seedless raisins
1 tablespoon ground cinnamon
¼ cup (½ stick) butter
½ teaspoon salt (optional)
2 teaspoons baking soda
¼ cup warm water
3 cups flour

Preheat oven to 325 degrees. Butter a 10-inch Bundt pan or a 9 × 5 × 3-inch loaf pan. Place water, sugar, raisins, cinnamon, butter, and salt in a saucepan. Mix well, bring to a boil, and cook over low heat for 15 minutes. Remove pan from heat, and cool slightly. Dissolve baking soda in warm water,

Theodor Uppman.

then add to pan. Add the flour and mix thoroughly. Pour batter into pan and bake 1 hour, 10 minutes. Remove cake from oven. Run a knife around the top edge of the pan to loosen the cake, then invert pan onto a cake rack to cool. *Important*: Wait until the next day to cut the cake. If well covered, cake will stay fresh for 3 weeks. *Serves about 8.*

Theodor Uppman
has sung nearly 400 performances of baritone roles at the Met, and created the role of Billy Budd in London. He and his wife, Jean, who is senior editor of the Annals of the Metropolitan Opera, *live in Manhattan. "The recipe for 'Three Weeks' Cake was given to Jean's mother by a neighbor, and has long been a favorite of both of us. During a family move the recipe was misplaced, and for twenty years we thought of it with great nostalgia. To our joy it turned up again, and it has fed our family and innumerable friends ever since. We once served it to Sam Barber, who ate two slices and later, when he had his coat on and was going out the door, said 'Do you suppose I could have just one more piece?' That cake did not last three weeks!"*

Michael Devlin
Pecan-Rum Pie

½ cup (1 stick) butter
Scant ¼ cup water
2 cups dark brown sugar
1 teaspoon vanilla extract
1½ tablespoons molasses
1 tablespoon rum, or to taste
3 eggs
1 9-inch unbaked pie shell (see page 213)
1¼ cups pecan halves

Preheat oven to 350 degrees. In a nonstick pan, combine butter, water, and brown sugar. Mix well and boil for about 3 minutes, until sugar is dissolved. Add vanilla, molasses, and rum, stir for a minute, then remove from heat. In a bowl, beat eggs with an electric beater. Slowly add the hot sugar mixture, beating constantly until well blended and smooth. Pour mixture into the pie shell. Top evenly with pecan halves. Bake for 40 to 45 minutes. Cool and store in the refrigerator until ready to serve. *Serves 6.*

Michael Devlin
who studied at Louisiana State University, came to sing at the Met in 1978. He has appeared in "Live From the Met" telecasts of Hansel and Gretel *and* Die Fledermaus.

Melitta Anderman
Melitta's Ladyfinger Cake

¼ cup (½ stick) butter
¾ cup confectioner's sugar
2 egg yolks, lightly beaten
⅔ cup strong coffee
1½ cups chopped walnuts
3 dozen ladyfingers
½ cup rum, approximately
1 teaspoon vanilla extract
1 pint heavy cream
1 (8-ounce) jar maraschino cherries, drained and
    dried

Cream butter and sugar, add beaten yolks, and blend well. Slowly add the coffee, stirring until smooth. Stir in nuts.

Separate the ladyfingers, then sprinkle with rum. Grease the bottom and sides of a 9-inch springform cake pan with removable bottom. Line the bottom with ladyfingers. Spread a thin layer of filling over the ladyfingers. Put in another layer of ladyfingers and filling, and continue until there are 3 or 4 layers, ending with ladyfingers. Cover the top of the cake with wax paper and weight down with a heavy plate. Refrigerate overnight.

To serve, remove wax paper and unmold the cake onto a platter. Stir vanilla into the cream and whip. Spread the

Licia Albanese and her son, Peppino.

whipped cream in a swirling motion over the cake. Decorate the cake with cherries, stems up. *Serves 4 to 6.*

Melitta Anderman is a secretary in the Met's Legal Department. She adds, "This cake is utter ecstasy . . . excellent with Champagne."

Licia Albanese
Ricotta Cheese Cake

2 cups sifted flour
1 cup (2 sticks) butter, softened
4 teaspoons sugar
½ cup sour cream
2 egg yolks
Grated zest of 2 lemons
¼ pound ricotta cheese, drained
¼ pound ground blanched almonds

Using your fingers, make a smooth dough of the flour, butter, 1 teaspoon sugar, 2 tablespoons sour cream, 1 egg yolk, and the grated zest of 1 lemon. Chill the dough for 1 hour.

Preheat oven to 350 degrees. Roll out the chilled dough to about ½ inch thickness. Use to line an 8-inch round cake pan. Blend the ricotta, 3 teaspoons sugar, 1 egg yolk, remaining sour cream, remaining lemon zest, and ground almonds

Licia Albanese.

until creamy. Pour filling into the pastry and bake until golden brown, about 45 minutes. *Serves 4 to 6.*

Licia Albanese sang at the Met for over twenty-five years, winning acclaim for her portrayals of Madama Butterfly, Mimi, Violetta, and many other roles. She lives in Manhattan with her husband, and continues to sing. An excellent cook, she notes that "All Italian girls must learn cooking. If I had the time, I think I could have a mano d'oro (golden hand) at cooking. But when you must hurry, everything burns. When I have something I must study well, I go to the kitchen and say to the cook, 'You set the table and I will cook.' "

Michel Sénéchal
Gâteau *La Dame Blanche*

Pastry

2 cups flour

6 tablespoons (¾ stick) butter

1 egg

2 tablespoons peanut or corn oil

Pinch of salt

2 tablespoons water

Filling

4–5 tablespoons apricot preserves or orange
  marmalade

1 scant cup confectioner's sugar

½ teaspoon vanilla extract

2 eggs, separated

¼ cup finely ground almonds or hazelnuts

5 tablespoons heavy cream

Prepare pastry first. In a bowl, combine flour, butter, egg, oil, salt and water. Mix quickly with your fingertips; don't overwork the dough. Chill for 1 hour.

Preheat oven to 350 degrees. Roll out dough and use it to cover the bottom of a 9-inch tart pan with a fairly high rim. Spread preserves or marmalade over the dough. Blend confectioners' sugar, vanilla, egg yolks, almonds, and cream. Stiffly beat the egg whites and fold in. Pour mixture into the tart pan and bake until golden brown, approximately 30 minutes. Check a few times during baking to be certain crust isn't browning too fast. Let cool, then cut. *Serves 6 to 8.*

Michel Sénéchal
came to the Met to play the four
tenor roles in the 1982 production of
Les Contes d'Hoffmann, *and has*
returned to sing in Le Nozze di
Figaro *and* Manon. *When sending*
us this recipe, he wrote, "This is an
old recipe from Rouen in Normandy,
birthplace of Boieldieu, the composer
of the opera La Dame Blanche.*"*

Ariel Bybee
Chocolate Mousse Pie

Pastry and Garnish

3 cups chocolate-wafer crumbs

1 cup (2 sticks) butter, melted

2 ounces semisweet chocolate, for leaves

1 pint heavy cream, whipped

Filling

1 pound semisweet chocolate

2 whole eggs

4 eggs, separated

1 pint heavy cream

6 tablespoons confectioner's sugar

Mix crumbs with melted butter. Pat into the bottom and up the sides of a 9-inch springform pan. Refrigerate for at least 1 hour.

In the top of a double boiler over simmering water, melt the chocolate for filling. Remove from heat, and cool for 10 minutes. With a wooden spoon, beat the whole eggs, one by one, into the chocolate, then add the egg yolks. Whip the egg whites until stiff. Whip the cream with the confectioner's sugar. Fold egg whites and whipped cream into the chocolate mixture. Pour into the pie crust and refrigerate.

Pick leaves from your garden that have a smooth texture and heavy veins; camelia or ficus leaves are the best. Wash and dry them thoroughly. In a double boiler, melt chocolate and spread on the underside of the leaves. Refrigerate until chocolate hardens. When ready to use, pull leaf off the chocolate coating, starting at the stem end. Frost the top of the cake with whipped cream, and pipe large rosettes around the sides and in the middle. Put a chocolate leaf in each rosette. *Serves 6.*

Ariel Bybee
has sung many mezzo-soprano roles
at the Met since making her debut in
1977 as Giovanna in Rigoletto.

Renata Scotto is fed by conductor Richard Karp, while Dominic Cossa, Rita De Carlo, and Daniele Barioni look on.

Joyce Castle
Mother's Pumpkin Pie

1¼ cups mashed cooked pumpkin, preferably
* freshly cooked*
¾ cup sugar
½ teaspoon salt
¼ teaspoon ground ginger
1 teaspoon ground cinnamon
1 teaspoon flour
2 eggs, lightly beaten
1 cup evaporated milk
2 teaspoons orange juice
1 9-inch pie crust shell (see page 213)

Preheat oven to 425 degrees. Blend pumpkin, sugar, salt, ginger, cinnamon, and flour until smooth. Add remaining ingredients and blend well. Pour mixture into pie shell, and bake for about 45 minutes. *Serves 6.*

Joyce Castle
was born in Beaumont, Texas. She
made her Met debut in 1986 in Die
Walküre.

Timothy Jenkins
Texas Pecan Pie

Crust

2 cups flour
¾ cup vegetable shortening
½ teaspoon salt
6 tablespoons ice water

Filling

4 eggs, lightly beaten
1 cup sugar
½ cup dark corn syrup
½ cup light corn syrup
1 teaspoon vanilla extract
¼ cup (½ stick) butter, melted
1 cup pecan halves

Prepare crust. Blend flour and shortening. Dissolve salt in cold water and sprinkle water over the flour mixture. Mix well. Chill dough for 30 minutes, then divide in half. Roll out one half to a ¼-inch thickness and use to line a 9-inch pie pan. Reserve second half for another pie or freeze for later use. (The secret of this tender pie crust is in dissolving the salt in the cold water.)

Preheat oven to 275 degrees. Combine eggs and sugar. Beat until smooth and light, then add syrups, vanilla, and melted butter. Beat well, and pour into prepared pie shell. Cover top with pecan halves. Bake until firm, about 45 minutes. Cool on rack. *Serves 6 to 8.*

Note This pie will not boil over in the oven.

Timothy Jenkins
made his Met debut in 1979, and
has since sung such tenor roles as
Parsifal, Siegmund, and Oedipus.
He studied at North Texas State
University, and still lives in
Amarillo.

OPPOSITE: *The Grand Tier Restaurant at the Metropolitan Opera, Lincoln Center.*

Judy's Favorite Chocolate Cookies
Judith Blegen

Viennese Chocolate Cookies
Mrs. Alexander Brand

Magnolia Dreams
Katharine T. O'Neil

Candied Pecans
Mrs. William Rogers Herod

Dolci Della Zia Glenna
David Hamilton

Maori Kisses
Kiri Te Kanawa

Confiture de "Vieux Garçon"
Michel Sénéchal

The Candy House in Hansel and Gretel. OVERLEAF:
*Kiri Te Kanawa's Maori Kisses, and the silver rose
used in her performances of* Der Rosenkavalier. *Dame
Kiri is shown as Arabella.*

COOKIES AND CONFECTIONS

Judith Blegen
Judy's Favorite Chocolate Cookies

½ cup (1 stick) butter
2 ounces unsweetened chocolate
1 egg
1 cup dark brown sugar
1½ cups flour
½ teaspoon baking soda
½ cup milk
1 cup chopped walnuts or pecans
1 cup confectioner's sugar

Preheat oven to 375 degrees. Generously grease a baking sheet. Melt butter and chocolate together in the top of a double boiler. Beat the egg and add brown sugar. Stir in the chocolate mixture. Sift flour with the baking soda, then add to batter, alternating with milk. Stir in nuts. Drop by teaspoonfuls onto baking sheet, leaving 2 inches between. Bake for 8 to 10 minutes. Let cookies cool on rack. Sift confectioner's sugar into a bowl and add milk drop by drop, stirring well, until you have a thick, spreadable glaze. Spread glaze on cookies and let set. *Makes about 2 dozen.*

*Judith Blegen
has sung more than 200 performances of nineteen roles at the Met,*
*including Gretel, Juliette, Adina,
Oscar, and Gilda. "This is my
mother's recipe, and I think they're
the best cookies in the world. You
can also add chocolate to the icing,
and then they're really wonderful!"*

Mrs. Alexander Brand
Viennese Chocolate Cookies

6 ounces German sweet chocolate
6 ounces shelled almonds
4½ cups flour
1½ cups (3 sticks) butter, room temperature
1½ cups sugar, plus additional for sprinkling
3 eggs; plus 1 egg for glaze, lightly beaten
¾ teaspoon baking powder
¾ teaspoon ground cloves
¾ teaspoon grated nutmeg
¾ teaspoon ground cinnamon

*From a Met
program,
1919.*

Crane's
Mary Garden Chocolates

*"Your Chocolates are really the finest I have
ever tasted anywhere in the World"*

Break chocolate into small pieces and freeze for several hours.

In a food processor fitted with the steel blade, grind almonds to the consistency of sugar. Remove almonds, then grind frozen chocolate to the same fineness, adding a tablespoon of flour to keep chocolate from melting. Set aside. Rinse and dry processor bowl.

Process butter, sugar, and 3 eggs until fluffy and lemon colored. Add almonds and chocolate, and blend. Sift together remaining flour, baking powder, cloves, nutmeg, and cinnamon. With processor running, add the flour mixture gradually to the ingredients in the bowl (see note). Put dough in wax paper, and freeze for several hours or overnight.

Preheat oven to 375 degrees. Butter 2 baking sheets. On a pastry cloth, roll out the dough until ⅛ inch thick. Cut into desired shapes with a sharp-edged cookie cutter and transfer to sheets. Glaze with beaten egg, then a sprinkling of sugar. Bake for 8 minutes. *Makes about 4 dozen.*

Note Depending on make and model, the processor may not take the whole amount of flour and may slow down or stop. In that case, turn the mixture onto a board and knead in the remaining flour.

Katharine T. O'Neil
Magnolia Dreams
DIVINITY

2⅔ cups sugar
⅔ cup light corn syrup
½ cup water
2 egg whites
1 teaspoon vanilla extract
1 cup finely chopped pecans

In a saucepan, heat sugar, corn syrup, and water until sugar is dissolved. Cook without stirring until it reaches 260 degrees on a candy thermometer (or until small amount dropped into very cold water forms a hard ball).

In a mixer bowl, beat egg whites until they form stiff peaks. Continue beating and pour hot syrup in a thin stream into the egg whites. Add vanilla and keep beating until mixture holds its shape and becomes slightly dull. Blend in chopped pecans. Drop mixture from the tip of a lightly buttered spoon onto wax paper. Let cool. *Makes about 4 dozen.*

*Katharine T. O'Neil
is a member of the Board of Directors
of the Metropolitan Opera Guild, a
Managing Director of the Metropolitan Opera Association, and is
Special Project Director for Lincoln
Center.*

Mrs. William Rogers Herod
Candied Pecans

2 cups (about 6 ounces) pecan halves
6 tablespoons sugar
1 cup peanut or corn oil

Place pecans in a saucepan and cover with water. Bring to a boil and cook for 5 minutes. Drain well. Put pecans back into the pan and add the sugar. Mix well; the melted sugar should evenly coat the pecans. Transfer the nuts to a plate, and spread out to dry for 10 minutes.

In a deep skillet, heat oil to about 325 degrees. Fry the pecans, 1 cup at a time, until the sugar coating has caramelized, about 4 to 5 minutes. Stir constantly so that the pecans are evenly fried. With a slotted spoon, remove to a large plate. Spread in a single layer to cool, then transfer to paper towels to absorb any excess oil. After cooling, the candied pecans can be stored in a jar or tin and remain crisp and crunchy for months. *Makes about 2 cups.*

Note Walnuts can be used instead of pecans.

Mrs. William Rogers Herod is a member of the Board of Directors of the Metropolitan Opera Guild.

David Hamilton
Dolci Della Zia Glenna
AUNT GLENDA'S CANDY

½ cup (1 stick) butter
2 pounds confectioner's sugar
3 cups coarsely chopped pecans
1 tablespoon vanilla extract
1 (14-ounce) can condensed milk
1 pound semisweet chocolate

In a large mixing bowl, combine all ingredients except chocolate and blend well. With lightly buttered hands roll mixture into small balls and place on wax paper. Melt chocolate in the top of double boiler over hot (not boiling) water. Cool for 2 minutes, then return to hot water. Place the candy balls, 1 at a time, on a teaspoon or skewer, dip into hot chocolate, and coat them. Store on layers of wax paper in airtight tins, preferably in refrigerator. *Makes about 3 dozen.*

David Hamilton notes that, "Aunt Glenda's Candy is a holiday tradition in our family."

Kiri Te Kanawa
Maori Kisses

Kisses

½ cup (1 stick) butter

about ⅔ cup superfine sugar

2 eggs

2 cups flour

2 teaspoons baking powder

1½ tablespoons unsweetened cocoa powder

1 cup chopped dates

1 cup chopped walnuts or pecans

Vienna Icing

½ pound confectioner's sugar (about 1¾ cups)

½ cup (1 stick) butter

1 tablespoon cream sherry

½ teaspoon vanilla extract

Preheat oven to 350 degrees. Lightly grease a baking sheet. In a bowl, cream butter and sugar. Add eggs and beat well. Sift together the flour, baking powder, and cocoa, then add to creamed mixture. Mix in dates and nuts. Drop the mixture in teaspoonfuls onto baking sheet, then flatten each slightly to about ½ inch thickness. Bake for 10 to 15 minutes.

Prepare icing while kisses cool. Sift the sugar. Cream butter, then while beating, gradually add half the sugar until creamy and fluffy. Beat in sherry and the remaining sugar. Stir in vanilla.

Remove kisses from baking sheet and join pairs of kisses together with icing. *Makes about 4 dozen.*

Note Some icing variations include:

Chocolate—Sift 1 tablespoon cocoa with the sugar.

Orange—Use 1 tablespoon orange juice and 1 tablespoon zest instead of sherry.

Coffee—Sift 1 tablespoon instant coffee with the sugar.

Walnut—Fold in 2 tablespoons finely chopped walnuts.

Liqueur—Use 1 tablespoon of your favorite liqueur instead of sherry.

Kiri Te Kanawa was born in Gisborne, New Zealand, and sang throughout Europe and in San Francisco before coming to the Met in 1974. She has since become one of today's most celebrated sopranos, and has appeared on "Live From the Met" in Der Rosenkavalier *and Die Fledermaus.*

Michel Sénéchal
Confiture de "Vieux Garçon"

1–1½ quarts white rum
1 vanilla bean, split in half lengthwise
6 cloves
1½ cups sugar
1 cup water
Fruits of the season: cherries, plums, apricots,
*   peaches, figs, etc.*

Put rum in a wide-mouth glass jar or crock with a tight-fitting lid. Add the vanilla bean and the cloves. Close tightly and let stand for several days.

In a saucepan, dissolve sugar in water. Let syrup simmer for a few minutes until clear and thick. Remove from heat, cool, then add to the jar with the rum and mix well.

As fruits come into season, wash them, dry carefully, and remove pits. Add to the jar, mix gently from time to time, and let stand for some time before serving plain or with ice cream. *Makes about 2 quarts.*

Note Do not use oranges, strawberries, currants, raspberries, or lemons.

On February 7, 1909, the musicians held a farewell dinner for Marcella Sembrich, who had sung over 400 performances with the Met since she starred as Lucia in the Met's second performance in 1883. Among those seen here in the Hotel Astor ballroom are (beginning in the left field) Andreas Dippel, Jan Paderewski, Madame Sembrich, Walter Damrosch, Antonio Scotti, Enrico Caruso, Victor Herbert, and Louise Homer.

Swedish (Semisweet) Rye Bread
Kathryn Perry

White Rice Muffins
Elaine Russell

Batyah's Pecan Rolls
Batyah Godfrey Ben-David

Zucchini Nut Bread
Rhona Ferling

Danish Kringla
Kathryn Perry

Tea Ring
Lotte Lehmann

Irish Soda Bread
Kay Long

OPPOSITE: *Tea at Bayreuth with the Wagners on August 23, 1881. Left to right are Richard Wagner; his wife, Cosima; Heinrich von Stein; Paul von Joukowsky; and Cosima's daughters, Daniela and Blandine von Bülow.* OVERLEAF: *Lotte Lehmann's Tea Ring, shown with a portrait of Madame Lehmann, a period libretto from* Der Rosenkavalier, *and Arturo Toscanini's pocket watch.*

SAVORY BREADS AND SWEET TEABREADS

Kathryn Perry
Swedish (Semisweet) Rye Bread

2 cakes yeast, or 4 packages active dry yeast
¼ cup warm water (105–115 degrees)
2 cups milk
1½ cups water
¾ cup molasses
¾ cup sugar
1 tablespoon salt
½ cup vegetable shortening
3 cups medium rye flour
6–7 cups all-purpose flour

Dissolve yeast in warm water. Bring milk to scalding point, then remove from heat. Combine with water, molasses, sugar, salt and shortening. Stir mixture until shortening is dissolved, then add yeast mixture and stir well. Gradually add rye flour to the mixture, stirring all the time, then blend in as much all-purpose flour as needed until dough is no longer sticky.

Knead well (about 10 minutes), then cover with clean cloth and let stand until doubled in bulk, about 1½ hours.

Punch down dough. Turn out onto a greased board or flat surface, roll out, and shape into 4 loaves. Put loaves in greased 9 × 5-inch baking or bread pans, lightly grease the tops of the loaves, and let rise again to double their bulk, about 45 minutes. Preheat oven to 350 degrees and then bake loaves for 45 to 50 minutes. Let cool somewhat before turning out of pans. *Makes 4 loaves.*

Kathryn Perry
is the Manager of the Guild's
Design Services Department, and
designs many of the Guild's publica-
tions, recordings, and promotions.

Elaine Russell
White Rice Muffins

½ cup soy flour
1½ cups white rice flour
¼ teaspoon baking soda
4 teaspoons baking powder
½ teaspoon salt
½ cup sugar
2–3 eggs, room temperature
½ cup small-curd cottage cheese
1 cup buttermilk
¼ cup (½ stick) butter, melted

Preheat oven to 350 degrees. Grease 12 muffin tins. Blend dry ingredients and set aside. Mix eggs, cottage cheese, buttermilk, and melted butter until smooth. Pour into the dry mixture and mix just long enough to moisten. Spoon batter into muffin tins and bake for 20 to 30 minutes. *Makes 12.*

Note These muffins can be frozen. Remove from freezer when ready to use, then pass very quickly under cold running water. Shake dry and place on a baking sheet. Reheat, uncovered, at 200 degrees for about 20 minutes. They'll come out as though freshly baked.

Elaine Russell
is the secretary for the Metropolitan
Opera Orchestra.

Batyah Godfrey Ben-David
Batyah's Pecan Rolls

1 cake fresh yeast, or 2 packages active dry yeast
¼ cup warm water (105–115 degrees)
1½ cups (3 sticks) butter, plus melted butter
½ cup sugar
3 eggs
½ cup sour cream
5–6 cups flour
1 cup milk
Pinch of salt
1 cup dark brown sugar
Pecan halves
Chopped walnuts
Raisins
Ground cinnamon

Dissolve yeast in warm water and let sit for 5 minutes, or until foamy. In a large mixing bowl, cream 1 cup (2 sticks) butter and the sugar. Add eggs, sour cream, and proofed yeast. Beat well. Slowly add flour, alternating with milk, to the batter. Add salt. Mix thoroughly until a soft ball of dough is formed. Place a towel over the bowl and refrigerate for 8 hours or overnight.

Lightly grease 24 muffin tins. Place 1 teaspoon of remaining butter and 1 teaspoon brown sugar in the bottom of each tin. Press pecans, rounded side down, on the sugar. Remove dough from refrigerator. Divide in half and roll out in two 1-inch-thick rectangles. Brush the rectangles with melted butter, then sprinkle with remaining brown sugar, chopped nuts, raisins, and cinnamon. Roll up the dough like a jelly roll, and cut each roll into 12 slices. Place a slice into each tin, on top of the pecan halves. Let the rolls rise until doubled in bulk, about 30 minutes.

Preheat oven to 375 degrees. Bake rolls until nicely browned, about 20 minutes. Turn out onto wax paper and let cool. *Makes 2 dozen.*

Batyah Godfrey Ben-David
made her Met debut in 1969, and
since then has sung many mezzo-
soprano roles for the company.

Rhona Ferling
Zucchini Nut Bread

3 eggs
1 cup vegetable oil
1 cup sugar
⅓ cup molasses
2 teaspoons vanilla extract
2 cups all-purpose flour
½ cup whole wheat flour
1 teaspoon salt
1 teaspoon baking soda
½ teaspoon baking powder
2 teaspoons ground cinnamon
2 cups shredded zucchini
1 cup raisins (see Note)
1 cup chopped nuts

Preheat oven to 350 degrees. Grease and lightly flour two 9 × 5-inch loaf pans. Beat eggs, oil, sugar, molasses, and vanilla until thick and foamy. Combine the dry ingredients, then add to the egg mixture and stir until just blended. Add zucchini, raisins, and nuts; mix gently. Fill pans with the mixture and bake for 1 hour. *Makes 2 loaves.*

Note Soak the raisins first in hot water for 5 minutes, then blot dry and coat lightly with flour. They will remain plumper and will stay evenly distributed in the batter instead of sinking to the bottom of the pan.

Rhona Ferling
was the Advertising Assistant for
Opera News.

Kathryn Perry
Danish Kringla
ALMOND PUFF

Pastry
2 cups flour
1 cup (2 sticks) butter
1½ tablespoons cold water
1 cup water
3 eggs
1 teaspoon almond extract
Sliced almonds, for garnish

Icing
1 cup confectioner's sugar
1 tablespoon heavy cream
1 tablespoon butter, softened
1½ teaspoons almond extract

Place 1 cup flour in a bowl and cut in ½ cup (1 stick) butter until mixture resembles coarse meal. Sprinkle in cold water and mix until dough cleans sides of bowl. Divide into 2 equal portions. On a baking sheet, pat out dough into two 4 × 5-inch strips.

Preheat oven to 350 degrees. Place water and remaining butter in a saucepan. Bring to a boil, then remove from heat. All at once, add the remaining flour and beat briskly until smooth. Then add eggs, 1 at a time, beating well. Add almond extract. Spread this mixture on the dough strips and bake for 45 to 55 minutes. Dough will rise like a cream puff, but fall a bit when cooled.

While pastry bakes, prepare icing. Blend ingredients well. When pastry is baked, remove from oven and sprinkle icing on puffs. Garnish with sliced almonds. Cut in diagonal strips for serving. *Makes 2 strips.*

ABOVE: *Richard Stilwell, Allan Monk, and José Carreras have little but bread and wine in this scene from* La Bohème.

Lotte Lehmann
Tea Ring

1¼ cups milk, scalded

½ yeast cake, or 1 package active dry yeast

3½ cups flour

¼ cup (½ stick) butter, melted

⅓ cup sugar

1 egg, well beaten

⅛ teaspoon salt

½ teaspoon almond extract

Sugar, ground cinnamon, and additional melted
   butter for glazing

Confectioner's sugar mixed with a little hot
   water, for icing (105–115 degrees)

Remove ½ cup of scalded milk and cool to lukewarm. Add the yeast and stir. When yeast is dissolved, add ½ cup flour, mix well, and let rise, about 15 minutes. When light and foamy, add the remaining milk and 2 cups flour. Stir until thoroughly mixed. Cover and let rise again, about 30 minutes. Add melted butter, sugar, egg, salt, almond extract, and ¾ cup flour. Toss on a floured pastry cloth and knead, using ¼ cup flour. Cover and let rise until doubled in bulk, about 1 hour.

Shape dough, using hands, and make a long roll. Put on an unfloured board and roll, using a rolling pin, until as thin as possible. Spread with melted butter, and sprinkle with sugar and cinnamon. Roll like a jelly roll. Cut roll in half. Trim each end and join ends to form 2 rings. Butter a baking sheet, then place the rings on sheets. Slash tops with scissors at 1¼-inch intervals, slanting from edge to within 1 inch of center. Spread the cuts 2 inches apart. Let rings rise until doubled in bulk, about 45 minutes. Preheat oven to 375 degrees, then bake for 30 minutes.

Ice with confectioner's sugar glaze. *Makes 2 rings.*

Lotte Lehmann sending a food package to post-war European refugees.

Lotte Lehmann (1888–1976)
*was a celebrated singer in Europe for
many years before making her Met
debut in 1934. She gave her farewell
concert in 1951, having sung for
more than forty years, and thereafter
taught singing in Santa Barbara,
California.*

Kay Long
Irish Soda Bread

*4½ cups flour
4 teaspoons baking powder
2 teaspoons salt
1 tablespoon caraway seed
1 (16-ounce) box raisins
3 cups milk
Butter, in pieces
3 tablespoons sugar mixed with 1 tablespoon
 milk*

Preheat oven to 350 degrees. Grease a 9-inch round cake pan. Sift together flour, baking powder, and salt. Mix in caraway seed and raisins, then add milk, stir, and blend well. The batter should be quite gooey. Pour into pan and bake for 1 hour, 15 minutes. The loaf should be light brown. Spread a few pats of butter on top. Mix sugar and milk and use to glaze the top of the bread. Cover with dish towel. Best served warm. *Makes 1 loaf.*

*Kay Long
is the Customer Service Representative for the Guild's Mail Order
Merchandising program.*

ABOVE: *Amelita Galli-Curci serving tea.*

PROP CREDITS

FRONT COVER: Mrs. August Belmont's brooch and opera gloves courtesy the Metropolitan Opera Guild Memorabilia Collection. Platter, bowl, fork, candlesticks, crystal, and salt cellars courtesy Tiffany & Co. Rabbits courtesy Roy Finamore. Linens courtesy Léron, Inc.

PAGES 18–19: *Fidelio* pistol courtesy the Metropolitan Opera Association. Plates, crystal, silver, and frame courtesy Tiffany & Co. Flowers courtesy Rhinelander Florist, Inc.

PAGES 42–43: *Lucia* dagger courtesy the Metropolitan Opera Association. Plates, candlesticks, frame, and crystal courtesy Tiffany & Co. Silver serving pieces courtesy James II Galleries Ltd. Linens courtesy Léron, Inc. Flowers courtesy Mädderlake.

PAGES 62–63: *Rigoletto* jester's stick courtesy the Metropolitan Opera Association. Tureen and soup plates courtesy James Robinson, Inc. All silver courtesy James II Galleries Ltd. Frame courtesy Tiffany & Co. Linens courtesy Françoise Nunnallé.

PAGES 78–79: *Butterfly* fan and comb courtesy Renata Scotto. Plates, frame, crystal, and flatware courtesy Tiffany & Co. Candlesticks courtesy James II Galleries Ltd. Porcelain flowerbasket courtesy James Robinson, Inc. Linens courtesy Françoise Nunnallé. Flowers courtesy Christatos & Koster, Inc.

PAGES 94–95: *Otello* sword courtesy the Metropolitan Opera Association. Plates, candlesticks, and salt cellar courtesy Tiffany & Co. Silver goblets courtesy James Robinson, Inc. Silver spoons and frame courtesy James II Galleries Ltd. Textile courtesy Françoise Nunnallé.

PAGES 110–111: *Carmen* comb and fan courtesy Regina Resnik. All other props courtesy Tiffany & Co. Wine courtesy Sherry-Lehmann, Inc.

Linens courtesy Léron, Inc. Flowers courtesy Rhinelander Florist, Inc.

PAGES 142–143: Tetrazzini veil courtesy the Metropolitan Opera Archives. Rossini cane handle courtesy the Metropolitan Opera Guild Memorabilia Collection. Plates and serving dish courtesy Mrs. Frank G. Lyon. Crystal and serving spoons courtesy James II Galleries Ltd. Flatware courtesy A la Vieille Russie, Inc. Frame courtesy Muriel Karasik. Linens courtesy Françoise Nunnallé. Flowers courtesy Rhinelander Florist, Inc.

PAGES 164–165: *Ballo* mask courtesy Roberta Peters. Plates, silver, and crystal courtesy Tiffany & Co. Frame courtesy James II Galleries Ltd. Salt and pepper shakers courtesy James Robinson, Inc. Flowers courtesy Rhinelander Florist, Inc.

PAGES 176–177: *Butterfly* scarf and *Aida* headband courtesy Lucine Amara. Dessert bowls, flatware, and crystal courtesy Tiffany & Co. Frame courtesy Muriel Karasik. Linens courtesy Françoise Nunnallé. Flowers courtesy Rhinelander Florist, Inc.

PAGES 176–177: *Butterfly* scarf and *Aida* headband courtesy Lucine Amara. Dessert bowls, flatware, and crystal courtesy Tiffany & Co. Frame courtesy Muriel Karasik. Linens courtesy Françoise Nunnallé. Flowers courtesy Rhinelander Florist, Inc.

PAGES 196–197: Callas *Butterfly* fan courtesy Nancy B. Duryee. Bellini watch courtesy the Metropolitan Opera Guild Memorabilia Collection. Plate and frame courtesy A la Vieille Russie, Inc. Flatware, cup and saucer, and cake plate courtesy Mrs. Frank G. Lyon. Gloves courtesy Hermès of Paris, Inc. Linens courtesy Françoise Nunnallé. Flowers courtesy Rhinelander Florist, Inc.

PAGES 226–227: Toscanini watch courtesy the Metropolitan Opera Guild Memorabilia Collection. Dessert plates, cups and saucers, and cake plate courtesy James II Galleries Ltd. Tea service courtesy Buccellati Silver Ltd. Sugar tongs courtesy James Robinson, Inc. Frame courtesy A la Vieille Russie, Inc. Flatware and cake trowel courtesy Mrs. Frank G. Lyon. Linens courtesy Françoise Nunnallé. Flowers courtesy Rhinelander Florist, Inc.

Flowers for cover photograph by Windflowers; all other flowers styled by Marjorie Kernan
Food stylist: Jeanne Marie Voltz
Photographer's assistants: Sergio Purtell and André Strong
Coordination: Lou Lou Horvath and Wendy Fanjul
Food photography directed by Bridget De Socio

SOURCES OF ILLUSTRATIONS

John Bechtold: 47
© 1988 Beth Bergman: 79 (Scotto as Cio-Cio-San), 95 (Domingo as Otello), 215
© 1988 Erika Davidson: 34, 62 (Milnes as Iago)
Henry Grossman: 109
James Heffernan: 81, 216 (Te Kanawa as Arabella)
Metropolitan Opera Archives: Front cover (Hempel), Back cover (Menu), 1, 6, 25, 28–29 (Sedge Leblang), 30, 61, 70, 93, 121 (Leblang), 122 (Leblang), 133, 135, 139 (Newspaper clipping), 155, 161, 175, 183, 195, 218
Metropolitan Opera Association: 80, 199
Metropolitan Opera Club: 38, 66
Metropolitan Opera Guild/Education Department: Front cover (Malas by William Harris), 7 (William Harris), 10–11 (Harris), 14–15 (Harris), 22 (Frank Dunand), 26–27 (Dunand), 39 (Wist Thorpe), 54–55 (Harris), 59 (Dunand), 106–107 (Harris), 119 (Dunand), 126–127 (Thorpe), 151 (Harris), 185 (Thorpe), 189 (Dunand), 231 (Harris)
Metropolitan Opera Guild/OPERA NEWS: Front cover (Patti; Ponselle), Back cover (Albanese; Pinza), 2–3, 4 (Alexandre Georges), 17 (Louis Reens), 18 (Nilsson as Brünnhilde by Louis Mélançon), 20, 21, 37, 41, 42 (Sutherland as Marie), 51, 52, 57, 58, 65, 68, 73, 74–75, 77, 85, 88, 104 (Gary Renaud), 110 (Resnik as Donna Anna), 116, 118, 124–125, 130, 141, 142 (Tetrazzini photo), 144, 153 (photo), 159, 163, 165 (Peters as Oscar by Mélançon), 172, 177 (Amara as Rosalinda by Mélançon), 186, 187, 188, 197 (Callas photo), 205, 208, 209, 211, 212, 222–223, 225 (Adolf von Gross), 226 (Lehmann photo), 232
New York Historical Society, courtesy of: 45 (from an engraving by Edvard Marcus)
Jarmila Novotná, courtesy of: 32
Vernon L. Smith: Back cover (Price), 102
Dorle Soria, courtesy of: 179, 200, 201, 203
The Family of Richard and Sara Tucker, courtesy of: Front cover, 192
Robert Tuggle Collection: 35, 72, 99, 137, 233
Mrs. Theodor Uppman, courtesy of: 207
Dan Wynn: 31, 67, 71, 83, 114, 115, 123, 158, 168

NAME INDEX

RECIPE INDEX

Designed by Jeff Batzli
Composed in Bembo by
Trufont Typographers, Inc.,
Hicksville, New York, and
in Bem by Arkotype Inc.,
New York, New York.
Printed and bound by Arnoldo
Mondadori Editore S.p.A.,
Verona, Italy.